Hummingbird in a Hurricane

A soul's search for peace
during
cancer treatment

Michele Ahlheim- Mellert

Janine Fallon- Mower

Anam Cara Press- Woodstock, New York

Table of Contents

Hummingbird Cover art: Barbara Mower- Lowenthal

Dedication

Without the people listed, this book could never have been, not because of their contributions to the content or their inspiration, or even their support. This book is dedicated to those whom without, I would not even be alive and this book would never have been.

First and foremost I dedicate this to my beautiful daughter Kerri Mellert. For hundreds of hours (most of them alone) spent in waiting rooms and hospital rooms while I went through four different treatment processes for my cancer. For the miles she drove getting me to doctors' appointments and hospitals for treatments, for basically putting her life on hold to be there for me. There are no words that can say what's in my heart, but it knows that without her I would not be here and there would be no book.

Then there are those incredible women who literally dropped everything to drive me to New York City (the one place my daughter cannot drive in). I am in awe of the kindness, love and support of Mary Ann Styles, Sheryl Wiener, Jessica Duffy Thibodeau Reynolds and Joan Pollard. Each of these wonderful women contributed to saving my life by the unselfish act of giving up a few hours driving me to NYC to Sloan Kettering and waiting for sometimes hours to drive me home.

Special thanks to Janice White, a woman whom I regard as a friend, sister, and daughter. You were there for me at the most unimaginably difficult times.

Last but not least my cousin Janine Fallon-Mower who took it upon herself to coordinate and edit each of these writings (which were originally posts on Face Book that I began when I was diagnosed with the cancer to keep me from going under) putting them together and then publishing them. Being an avid historian she has written three books on the history of our hometown and her husband's family and their part in our history. And lastly, reviewing these posts was, I paid no attention to spelling or punctuation, I just wanted to get those thoughts down.

Thank you all, I love you and am eternally grateful………………

Shelli

Preface

Hummingbird in a Hurricane is a book whose inception began on FB. In the posts, Michelle shares her personal thoughts and feelings that are generated during her diagnosis and treatment of melanoma skin cancer. My thoughts and feelings come from the prospective of the observer of a loved one who is experiencing a new life with cancer.

Baby boomers either love or hate social networking. Michelle, a.k.a. Shelli. and I embraced Facebook (FB) in 2009. My reasoning was twofold, to keep up with activities of family and my grandchildren while also promoting the Mower's Saturday Flea Market in Woodstock with a FB page. Shelli jumped into the FB community to reconnect with old friends and to explore the untapped universe of the Internet. I think it is safe to say that now, web surfing and social networking is incorporated into both our daily lives. Most of the experiences have been positive and beneficial.

As would be expected, we both had a level of privacy concerns about sharing bits of our life experiences on the web and in the social networking arena. We came of age during the 1960's. The sexual revolution was in full swing, and many times we relied on our youthful wisdom, some sort of protection to guard against pregnancy and our ability to assess people's intentions to shield us from any untoward problems. It is safe to say that while using social networking media in the 21st century, we now use a similar approach while surfing the internet. We hope that the wisdom of age, a good virus protect program and astute networking skills will protect us from any unpleasant experiences. The resultant risk taking provides a platform for a greater sharing and broader outreach of life experiences.

Through Shelli's writing, the reader can sense how those with a cancer diagnosis often develop a unique view of the time left to them in the physical realm. What emerged for me while reading her daily posts over a year or so was her gift of writing about her philosophy of life. When the diagnosis of melanoma skin cancer presented itself, Shelli's postings became not only a way for FB friends to be updated on her cancer treatment, but for all her followers to be given the gift of her insights as how, as she would

6

write, "Everyone is on a journey, traveling at different speeds".

When I discovered that Shelli had no hard copy record of her FB posts, I decided to randomly copy and paste them into a word document. Eventually, I realized that her posts were developing into a journey of hope and a search for peace during the whirlwind of activities that accompany cancer treatment. Shelli was writing about the emotional ups and downs of diagnosis and treatment. I found that she very aptly put into words the challenges and changes a person with a cancer diagnosis experiences in their home life, their personal friendships and social connections.

While in the middle of treatment, Shelli created a *"Today I am Grateful For"* FB page. Over the past three years, her "Grateful" page has grown to over five hundred followers, many of whom are residing in places that are thousands of miles from Woodstock. Each individual who posts shares her philosophy of speaking about what they are grateful for, no matter how insignificant the action or item may be. People who post adhere to the belief that the process of acknowledging what one is grateful for results in creating for each individual an aura of goodness and well being.

When I read her post of February 12, 2014 exclaiming "what an incredible life this is", I realized that Shelli postings needed to be shared beyond FB. As readers follow along, Shelli will, in a loving but frank manner, take them along on her journey into the land of cancer survivorship. This is a journey that includes traveling through fear and self doubt, crossing the desert of abandonment and negotiating the raging rivers of cancer treatment. All of these obstacles were met while navigating by the light of an inner beacon of universal love.

I sincerely thank Shelli for allowing me to bring her enriching and heartfelt work out of the social networking realm into a published book that readers can curl up with while relaxing and taking a respite from the hectic pace of modern life.

We hope that readers will return to this book over and over for encouragement and comfort, especially when the random act of opening to a page by chance, may lead to just the right inspiration needed for the day.

Janine Fallon- Mower, RN, BSN, Patient Navigator.

Staff Nurse, Fern Feldman Anolick Breast Center

Nurse Case Manager, 4SMC Oncology Floor,

Nurse Case Manager. 3 West telemetry/stroke floor.

Health Alliance, Kingston NY.

Introduction

Shelli Ahlheim -Mellert

A few years ago Hurricane Irene came up the east coast and we found ourselves in the midst of torrential rains and extremely high winds. I stood at our front door watching huge trees bend to the ferocity of Mother Nature. As I stood there in the throes of so many emotions I noticed a tiny hummingbird going about her business totally oblivious of the barrage surrounding her.

What amazing feats of nature were playing out before me! Huge trees were humbly bowing to the power of the blowing wind while a tiny hummingbird continued to fly about totally unaffected by the same wind. Common sense was telling me that little bird should have been slammed up against the side of the house, at the least, and yet there she was zooming about looking for the feeder we had brought in to keep it from being destroyed by the storm.

That tiny little bird became my mentor. She showed me that it is indeed possible to stay calm and continue doing what we need to when all around us is chaos and confusion. I realized it was not only possible but what we are meant to do. Part of our job on this journey we call life, is to understand that we have within us all that is needed to sustain us and keep us going despite appearances to the contrary. My journey began with a diagnosis of malignant melanoma, which resulted in surgery on my heel and subsequent amputation of my left leg above the knee after reoccurrence of the cancer.

I have been blessed with remission and now am concentrating on learning how to live life as an amputee and walk with a prosthetic. I think of that tiny bird often, if she can continue on her journey calm and focused in the midst of a hurricane then I can learn to walk without any aides despite neuropathy in my foot and hands from the chemo, arthritis in my knee and hip on the right side and some shoulder problems due to a glitch in my rotator cuff, for I truly am "A Hummingbird in a Hurricane"

Introduction

Janine Fallon- Mower

If you look at our family tree, you will learn that Shelli and I are first cousins. We have a special sister like relationship-essentially we have developed a deep life long friendship that is between two women who happen to be related.

Shelli was kind enough to agree to help me with the day care of my twin grandchildren who were born in 2009. Before you knew it, we set up a routine spending every Wednesday with Liam and Julia. We able to use the time the twins spent napping as time to relax together and continue the lively ongoing conversations we like to engage in about the origins of life, God, peace, aliens.... You name it, - no topic is off limits.

When Shelli showed me what she called a wound that would not heal, on her left heel, I admit I had no idea what it could be. My best suggestion was to visit the local wound center and let them have a look. Thankfully, an experienced podiatrist there thought to biopsy the skin and it was determined that Shelli had melanoma skin cancer on her left heel.

Thus began a journey, for me, of growing comfortable with feeling totally helpless. At the same time, I wanted to remain supportive of Shelli and hopeful about treatment and survival of melanoma skin cancer. As the disease progressed, and her necessary treatments required her to travel to Memorial Sloan Kettering (MSK) or Yale- New Haven (YNH), our face time became less and less. We began to keep in touch more and more on FB.

Coincidentally, as Shelli was entering into her experience with melanoma skin cancer, my younger brother was deep into the layers of treatment available for, coincidentally, metastatic melanoma skin cancer. A mole which had been present on his chest wall for much of his life was diagnosed as melanoma in 2009. Without going into to much scientific detail, Shelli and my brother, Jack, had different types of melanoma cells and science and medicine was actively throwing everything it had at my brother's cancer. It was quite an unsettling time for me, to say the least.

With two people whom I cared deeply about now fighting for their lives, I entered into a phase of life where I became melanomaphobic.

Each day I had to navigate the fear that would crop up in my mind if I saw what I thought was a new little discolored anomaly on my skin. I was fortunate that I was able to have Shelli's posts to read during this time, and the posts became a grounding or foundational activity for me during the last year of my brother's life. Everything that was familiar to me was changing as my brother's illness progressed.

In order to steady the rocky boat, I needed a beacon of hope to concentrate on. Shelli and her words, generated from her own cancer journey, became a light to focus on. Having a foundational belief in something greater than ourselves, I believe, is an essential tool to be used by people who are diagnosed with cancer. I have chosen as my foundational belief, God. However, any spiritual practice that leads one to the goal of acceptance in a setting of unconditional love can generate the same result. Acceptance, blanketed with unconditional love, provides a safe foundation from which to fight for ones life.

It is important to say that the same tool, resting in acceptance and a greater universal force of love, can also be utilized by friends and family members of people experiencing cancer.

Shelli, in a very organic and raw manner, writes about her

spirit or her soul's fears during the early days of diagnosis and treatment. It was very evident to me that during this process, her writing topics changed and what emerged was a hopeful acceptance of her new life with cancer.

It occurred to me that if sharing Michelle's story of courage could help one person who is facing a cancer diagnosis, then the time preparing this booklet would be well spent. And, if the parallel story of how Michelle's cancer diagnosis affected me can gives strength to family members of cancer survivors, then, perhaps people will be more likely to embrace loved ones with cancer instead of shying away from them at time of diagnosis.

What follows is a brief three year snapshot of hundreds of FB posts written by Shelli. Each year begins with an introduction written by me, which serves as an example of the balance that can be struck between the cancer survivor and their friends and loved ones.

Observations by Janine 2012

Shelli is now less able to spend time with the twins and me due to chemo related fatigue. We've enlisted the help of another close friend, Kathy, to lend a hand with twin care on Wednesdays. There are also the emotional and physical demands of travel for treatment that she must contend with. Shelli had undergone a wide excision of the left heel tumor that required hospitalization at MSK.

Eventually, the tumors would reoccur around the incision line. Yervoy, (ipilimumab) the most promising immunotherapy treatment for melanoma was proposed as an option and Shelli began the course of treatment with the usual trepidation one would expect to have when stepping down a dark unknown path. Fortunately, she was able to receive the ipilimumab at a local oncologist office. This is such an important development in cancer treatment for those of us living in the Hudson Valley- the coordination of treatment between a major cancer center and local oncologists!

Once it was determined that the ipilimumab was causing her liver enzymes to be elevated, the drug was stopped. There was also evidence that the cancer cells were not responding, as new tumor growth was observed at the incision line on Shelli's heel. Damn it, Damn it, were the first words that came to my mind.

In August of 2012, it was suggested that she go into treatment with Interleuken 2. (IL2). This is a cytokine signaling molecule of the human immune system and is part of the arsenal in the battle against melanoma. The thinking is that if you boost the immune system, it will begin to recognize the cancer cells as foreign invaders and attack them. Shelli, though preferring to be of the opinion that prayer and natural methods would cure her cancer, wholeheartedly embraced contemporary melanoma treatment and adds it to the bank of weapons that are being used to kill the cancer cells in her body. This treatment would eventually be administered at the Smilow Cancer Center at YNH.

Receiving IL2 is no simple undertaking. While Shelli is preparing herself for a one week stay at Smilow, for close observation while the IL 2 is being administered, I am having flashbacks of listening to my brother tell me his experience of receiving the same treatment. He received most of his treatments at NYU Langone/Perlmutter Cancer in Manhattan. The best way to describe how his voice sounded during treatment was; weak, strained, and scared.

He would later say that the IL2 knocked the crap out of him; he thought he was going to die during the treatment. I was left wishing the IL2 had knocked the crap out of his melanoma. I chose not to share any of this with Shelli. Shelli would endure two IL2 treatments at YNH. Her daughter Kerri took time off from work to stay by her mother's side during treatment. Using Shelli's own words, "It was pretty rough". During the second round of treatment Shelli was transferred into the ICU as her blood pressure bottomed out. Cancer treatment seems to require that the person tease death in order to cheat death.

My family and I miss spending time with Shelli. Days run into weeks, weeks run into months. Work schedules collide with treatment schedules. Facebook becomes our main communication method.

My brother Jack died on August 16, 2012 at Calvary Hospital in the Bronx. I remember being the observer at his burial, watching Shelli embrace my brother's daughter Kelly, both of them sobbing. I remember thinking, how unimaginably difficult this must be for Shelli.

Shelli's posts in 2012 represent the struggles she faces on a very personal level, however they echo sentiments that we all express as a result of the various stressors we encounter in our human lives.

POSTS

May 31, 2012

To stay connected to spirit when living in a physical world is the biggest challenge we will ever meet. I wake up in the morning (and immediately give thanks that I have indeed woken up again) I swing my feet over the side of the bed, sit up and there they are (the tumors) mocking me, daring me to not freak out challenging me to give in and just crawl back under the covers and let them take over. They have invited others to join them so there is a new lump to feel, see, look at, and worry about. I bless them, I acknowledge that God is everywhere, even in this appearance of cancerous tumors, I cover them up and I go about my day. Some days I don't go very far, I hang out in my chair in my jammies, but sometimes I just don't feel like putting on those hot stockings, and sometimes I feel tired so I just chill. Whatever challenge you are facing, I challenge you to wake up in the morning and face what I face every day. (and as big a challenge as this is, there are others who face even bigger ones, so I give thanks for the good things I do have and experience) It's not easy and I am so blessed to have the option.

June 5, 2012.

A perfect example of letting your ego get the best of you. Me. I almost got scammed into spending unnecessary money because someone out there is slimy enough to realize that there are people who feel the need to be validated in the things that they do. I write poems, and I fell into the trap of wanted to be validated, wanting someone to tell me they are good, that I have talent, that they are more then the ramblings of a crazy old lady.

My first reaction was hooray, then I started looking into things and found a lot of negative feedback about this group that holds this so called poetry contest. So I did send the form back allowing them to "publish" the poem, but I didn't order the book and I didn't pay to have a biography added. The books are for sale on Amazon. The bottom line I guess is, I checked my ego at the door, it was nice to think that "professionals" thought my work was good and having my poem published in a "questionable" publication doesn't matter. I write them cause it's what I feel, I have a blog if you'd like to read them, if not, it doesn't matter, they still make me happy.

June 6, 2012

We have been told from day one to "love our neighbor". Unfortunately we get hung up on the definition of love. For many love equals the romantic heart skipping palm sweating do anything to please you feelings we get. Others equate it to the love we feel for family and friends which truthfully I cannot put into words. What I do know is neither one of those can be projected on a perfect stranger. So...........how can we love our neighbors? Simply put, wish them well, hold no ill feeling toward them and bless them as a child of God. It will work with anything. Have pests in the house, wish them well, bless them and explain that it is not comfortable to be living in the same space and ask them to find another place to live (I say this because I recently read an article about a man who did this with a snake who decided to take up residence in the mans home, he would leave the door open hoping the animal would go but he didn't until the man wished him well and blessed him as he explained they were not meant to live in the same space) You don't have to "like" everyone to love them. But you do have to love everyone to live as we were meant to........

June 7, 2012

One of the more difficult parts of this journey is the loss of friends and sometimes even loved ones. I'm not talking about physical death, but of a parting of the ways. When friendships fall to the wayside it is because we have achieved a level that they have not. The methods they leave may seem harsh sometimes but the Universe knows what has to be done to make us let go. We need to make room for those who are travelling at the speed that we have achieved. Hold no ill will to those who must leave but bless them and know, you will meet again...............

June 9, 2012

Just reading a book does not make you intelligent. Reading hundreds of books doesn't either. You need to retain what you are reading and then put it to use. An important part of our journey is to put into practice what we learn. If we don't, it's just stored knowledge that is stagnant and going nowhere. If you don't put into practice what you "believe" how do you know if it fits right? You will fail, a lot, but the important thing is to be and active participant in your faith.........whatever it is.

June 12, 2012

There are times when your inner being is trying to tell you something and you just don't get it. The world doesn't feel right, or you may feel like you're in your body sideways. Things just aren't meshing like they should, or you feel compelled to do something but you don't know what. These are times of change that are coming from deep within, and can be very uncomfortable. We need to recognize them for what they are and slow down. Spirit will work at its own pace and we cannot force it or hurry it up. The most helpful thing is to stop trying to appease these feelings with outer remedies. It's kinda like trying to treat an ulcer with topical cream, it aint gonna work. Instead of running hither and yon, slow down; be more aware of what you inner self is saying. It wont necessarily make these times easier, but they will be less frustrating when you realize that ego based activities are not what the answer is. Give spirit time and room to do its thing.

June 14, 2012

Then God said, "Let us make mankind in our image, in our likeness..................

Has anyone ever questioned the fact that this say OUR image and OUR likeness?

However you interpret these words there is on thing that remains the same. Whether you believe it is speaking about the physical body or the spirit within if you believe in a creator then you must understand when you say I AM you are praying. You are declaring that this image that was created is sick, healthy, fat, thin, pretty, ugly, rich, poor . We know how powerful words are, the two most powerful words are I AM. Whatever you think God is when you say I am you are declaring that God is and you will find it in your world. Thoughts are powerful and able to create, words even more powerful and able to create. Be mindful of what comes into your head and what goes out of your mouth........................

June 15, 2012

Have you ever been stalled from doing something because you feel "I'm only one person, what difference can I make?" ? Uhhhhhh, Jesus (one person) , Buddha (one person), Mother Theresa (one person), Schindler (one person) Hitler (yes I'm including him because he was one person and look what he did!), Dali Lama (one person), the list is endless. The I'm only one person excuse just doesn't cut it. Live as if your every move will have the butterfly effect, you every word will impact someone, your every thought will manifest into the physical, for in reality these are truths that we must realize and take responsibility for.

June 17, 2012

Did you remember to slow down and stop to smell the roses today? Every moment affords us an opportunity to just slow down and be in that moment. Savor a sweet memory, watch the sun dance off the leaves, smile at the squirrels as they play tag in the branches, listen to the different songs of the different birds, let your imagination soar with hawk, tune in to the beauty and opportunity around you, the world is always speaking to us, learn to listen.

25

June 18, 2012

Working for the things that matter the most, are the things that don't make you any money. In fact, many times, these activities will possibly stop someone from making money ie saving the rain forests. No one pays you to save the whales, or the forests, or clean water, or to insure that no more of the creatures we share this planet with go extinct, but those activities are the only ones that truly matter. People are hungry, yet tons of good food is thrown out every day! What is it going to take for us to understand that any of the ego driven activities are destroying not only us but the world we live in? Pretty soon humans will be on the endangered species list who will save us??????????? Get out of you ego driven mind set and understand we are all one and we are indeed our brothers keeper.....................

June 19, 2012

Does anyone remember this episode of the Twilight Zone, does anyone remember the Twilight Zone???? The story was about an unassuming man who just wanted to be left alone to read his books, he gets his wish, he's the only person left on earth and he's surrounded by his beloved books......................he breaks his glasses. How often do we receive what we wanted only to have a monkey wrench thrown into the mix? Because we look to the outside for our happiness, we depend on physical things and events to make us happy, we let our ego determine if we're happy or sad. Until we learn that our happiness comes only from within, we will continue to get to the library only to have our glasses broken.

June 20, 2012

In my observations of life, I've notice a disturbing trend. People are reluctant to ask for help because they don't want to "owe" anyone. Does this stem from the fact that we tend to "keep score"? Life is NOT a game to keep score of. 99% of the good we do is not returned by the receiver but by someone or something else. Keeping score stifles the flow of energy and love that the Universe functions on. This is not to say you should become a doormat or let people take advantage of you cause, unfortunately, there are those out there who will, but you should not cut yourself off either. The Universe finds it's balance on it's own, trust in its knowledge of itself, reach out when you need to, respond when you should and never, ever, make it a game of keeping score! Keep in mind the ego is the scorekeeper of life.

June 25, 2012

Sometimes we grow weary. So bone tired that it seems like drawing the next breath is to much effort and doing anything is out of the question. We may be labeled as depressed, or with chronic fatigue or any number or other maladies, and in many cases this may be true, but............for some of us, we are just pushing to hard for the Universe to do what we want in our time frame. The harder we push, the further away our desires go, we cannot will the Universe to do our bidding. When we practice a life of gratitude and positive thinking it's like placing an order through a catalog. We wouldn't run to the mailbox the next day and expect our order to be there. We know it takes time to reach its destination, time to process and ship and we wait faithfully expecting it, not going crazy running to the mailbox every 10 minuets. No matter how much we think we know what is good for us and when we should get it, we don't. Place your order and have faith in the Celestial Post Office.

August 20 2012

When you continually do the right things, act in love and forgiveness and still continue to experience hardship and heartbreak you may begin to question the law of reaping what you sow. And here is where the law of Karma raises its ugly head.

It stands to reason if we are eternal forms of energy we would be constantly moving through lifetimes learning and evolving. Even scientists realize for every action there is an equal and opposite reaction. We tend to go through life either denying or totally oblivious to the fact that every thing we think, do and say sends out a vibration and causes "something" to happen. So when you up to you eyeballs in stuff that you don't think you deserve, perhaps not in this lifetime but in another you still have a debt to pay so continue to believe in the good, love unconditionally, and pay your debt so you can grow and prosper.

August 21, 2012

I have always been an advocate of embracing our inner child. Learning to see the world through the eyes of a child and interact with it with the awe and wonder of one who is experiencing it for the first time is a joy only those who have experienced it can understand.

But, as will all things in life, there is an opposite side to the coin.

There will be times when this child surfaces as the insecure,

frightened, needy persona and we must learn that it's okay to feel

that way as long as we let the "older" child dominate.

We spend our lives trying to ignore, stifle or even destroy the child,

when in fact no matter how long we are on this earth we are still

children. If you've , as an "adult", have never felt a twinge of fear in

the dark, longed for someone to just hold you and tell you everything

is ok, or just wanted to be tucked in bed and kissed goodnight, you're

lying to yourself and ignoring that child within. We perceive these

traits as weak and fight to not feel them and look down upon those

who do. It's ok, to be that frightened child once in a while, and if

you're lucky you have someone who on some level understand this

and will hold your hand in the dark or hug you and tell you its all

going to be ok. Our job is to strike a balance with the different stages

of childhood that dwell within us and to understand that 6 or 60 we

are still children and have a whoooole lot yet to learn.

August 25, 2012

We live in the cocoon of the human body, trained to depend on the physical to tell us where, what, who and how we are. In the journey of spirit when you go within you begin to see you are "unplugging" from the physical, beginning to understand that what you are feeling is not you. You freely say and understand "So this is what it's like to feel tired," knowing it is not you that is tired but the being you have created in the outer, you stop depending on what your senses are telling you, knowing that nothing can disturb the perfect spirit child you are. Then, slowly, like a butterfly the metamorphosis begins and then your spirit butterfly emerges.

August 26, 2012

No matter whom you are or what your beliefs, everyone comes to a point where they fall to the wayside. What's going on around us is just so overwhelming that we question the reality of our faith and if we're just "farting in a mitten" as it were. AA has a wonderful solution for these times "One day at a time". Just for today I can stay in faith despite the chaos around me. Just for today I can continue to believe in the love of the universe even though those around me are angry and unkind. Just for today I can see the miracles that exist around me and know that nothing is impossible when I have faith. Just for today I will let go and Let God knowing that whatever "God" is to me it is sustaining and maintaining me in love, peace, joy, health and abundance.

August 31, 2012

And so another bend in the road.........................

I was scheduled for my first treatment in the clinical trial yesterday, the doctor called me on Monday to inform me that the liver enzymes from the last treatment disqualified me from this trial. I cannot express the devastation................it took so much for me to get the courage to say "yes" and then scrambling to try to find rides to Manhattan not to mention the schedule rearranging my daughter did so she could go with me.

They now are recommending a treatment that is currently being used, but they want me to go to the hospital @ Harvard because they are supposedly the best equipped to administer this stuff and deal with any side effects. This would involve a 5 day hospital stay. OMG !!!!! In the mean time I'm going the herbs, supplements and diet route. I'm banking on this being a good thing and the alternative therapy will work and I won't have to do any of the crappy stuff..

Sept 1, 2012

I sat in my backyard today and just got overwhelmed by nostalgia, a yearning for what used to be, the person I was, the possibilities that lay before me. I wanted to be surrounded by friends laughing and having some fun cocktails and just enjoying life. I so wanted to push a magic button and make it all better. Then I remembered, when looking back we tend to remember the good stuff and forget the bad stuff. Fighting what is, is like trying to catch the wind. A waste of time and energy. I have met some of the most amazing people on this journey and made some wonderful friends that will be here for me, no matter what. Nostalgia has its place, and it's a nice place to visit, but don't set up housekeeping there, you will miss all the miracles that are going on around you. Accept today for what it is, embrace it, savor it and ....then..............let it go.

September 3, 2012

Taking responsibility for ourselves and our actions is a task few are willing to take on. When you speak words of hate towards an entire group of people because of the actions of a few, are you willing to take responsibility for spreading fear and hate to everyone in that group? Hate and prejudice are learned and who is responsible? Every disparaging remark plants a seed somewhere. We refuse to look at ourselves and understand that it's our fault. The hate, the fear, the intolerance, all of it, it didn't just come out of nowhere; it came from our mouths, our thoughts, stemmed from our fears. We have been doing this from day one, isn't it about time to realize that it isn't working? If we are to continue as a race, we must learn to live alongside of one another and accept and embrace our sameness and our differences. Respect one another and understand that underneath it all we are one and if you're sending out hate to someone you are in reality sending it to everyone, including yourself. And have no doubt, it will show up at your door. Take the responsibility of your actions, be the candle in the window, welcome everyone......

September 4, 2012

If you doubt the power of laughter, go for days without any at all, not a smile or a giggle let alone a good hearty gufaw and then finally find that laughter. I think the sound of laughter is just as much of a hymn as those we sing in churches. Something happens both physically and spiritually when you find your laughter. Never ever lose the ability to laugh. If there is nothing around you that makes you laugh, learn to laugh at yourself. My flaws, shortcomings and faux paxs have been a source of wonderful laughs over the years. By no taking yourself to seriously you open the door to be able to laugh at yourself, and laughter is indeed the "best medicine." You also get the added benefit of taking away any ammunition that others may chose to use against you when you laugh at yourself, admit your flaws, and don't take yourself to seriously, it eliminates a whole bunch of ammunition for those who are on a lower vibration.

September 6, 2012

Sometime the pressures of this world seem just to much to bear. We look around and we can see is troubles and sorrow, everyone you know is dealing with some kind of personal crisis and you have your own as well and there seems to be no way out, no place to find peace, nothing to be happy about and finding something to be grateful for is an unobtainable feat. That's when we need to remember the lowly lump of coal. It bears the weight of tons and tons of pressure for millions of years, it doesn't fight it, it doesn't try to get away from it, it doesn't try to change it, it just accepts what is......and then one day that lump of coal emerges as a beautiful gem. Bright, shiny, rare and the strongest material known to man. So the next time you're feeling overwhelmed by the pressures of life, remember that they are working on your inner sleeping spirit, who, if you allow the process to go it's course, will emerge as a shining rare gem and take its place in the crown of the universe.

September 7, 2012

No matter how unfair, unreasonable or cruel it seems there is the reality that there are those out there who can "throw the switch" as it were and change your direction. Our job is to not see it as an obstacle but rather an opportunity. The new direction is where we are supposed to go and will take us where we're supposed to be. It may not be where we think we want to be, but it's where we need to be at this point in our journey. Over the past couple of weeks I have had a few direction changes, and so have those around me. They have been disappointing and it's really hard for me to accept that it is as it should be because I cannot see the end result and it isn't where I wanted to go. Again, the epic struggle between the "ego self" who feels it knows all and is the best equipped to map my journey, and the spirit self who does know the outcome and is truly looking out for my best interest, and those around me. And so my goal today is to shake off the disappointment of where I was going and face the new road with anticipations and gratitude.

September 8, 2012

Today I am grateful for: the sense of smell, I notice the subtle changes in the air as the curtain of summer slowly closes and sense "fall in the air"; the ability to turn over and go back to sleep if the mood strikes me; not having to live "by the clock" anymore, my time is my own to do with as I please...........or to do nothing............

How many times during the course of a day, of a week, do you do what you "want" to do instead of what you feel you have to, should, are obligated or just habitually do? Can you, just do something you want to just because you want to, or do you feel guilty and selfish? Learning to take that time for us is a testament to faith. A moment of "letting go and letting God'. When you take that moment to just enjoy life, instead of trying to run it you are giving power back to the universe where it belongs. You are trusting that things will get done as they should when they should for the good of all, without you're help. We were given life to enjoy and savior, not to piddle away trying to force it's course. Your world will not come

38

crashing down around you if you take a half hour to sit and read a book , work on a craft project, enjoy the wonders of nature, or just sit quietly and meditate. As with all things we must strike a balance, which includes me time, a conscious letting go of the egos quest to run things and a complete giving over to the universe trusting it's love, wisdom and power.

September 12, 2012

I was doing some research on cancer and cancer treatments on the internet last night and what I found made me very sad. The one article was about thinking positive and having a positive attitude and it basically trashed the whole concept. I know from experience that it helps. It may not have directly affected the disease itself (we'll never know, maybe if I hadn't adopted the positive attitude things would have been much worse then they are), but it definitely has helped me navigate these choppy waters. It's a struggle and some times I just want to give in to the fear and morbid thoughts that sneak into my head. It's so much easier to do that, but by NOT giving in and making an effort to be positive and have faith my life has had a much better quality than someone who is in the "cancer mode". Taking control of my thoughts has given a sense of power in my life when there really is very little I have any control over. Chose what you will believe, and try things out before dismissing them just because someone says it won't work, or it does work. I don't expect anyone to just believe this just because I've written it, but I would hope that some would take the challenge and try to live a life of positive thinking, attitudes and love.................

September 13, 2014

Today I am grateful for: FB it has been an incredible experience for me, I have met some extraordinary people and it has given birth to this page and given me an outlet for my inner self; that I don't believe everything I read and only half of what I see; I have been able to stay relatively sane this past two years because of family and friends who have supported, loved and tolerated me when I do lose it.................

September 14, 2012

Today I am grateful for: all the incredible people who devote their lives to helping cancer patients, from the crazy man who led us to where we needed to go, to the doctors who take time explain things to you, to the social worker who maintained her cool when I squealed "Oh , she's just a baby!" when she walked in the door; to have the opportunity to walk along the beach with my daughter; to see so much positive coming from the simple concept of this page.......................

September 16, 2012

I feel like I've scratched this itch before, interview with the doctor at YNH, more of the same tests to do (although they did throw a new one at me this time a heart stress test in case my heart has any problems that would make it not a good idea to do this treatment) a total meltdown, stress, anxiety and fear about this upcoming ordeal, bouncing back and regrouping, extremely tired but so grateful for the little side trip my daughter and I took to the beach. Just the few moments walking along the beach and picking up a couple of seashells and sitting for a bit and taking in the breathtaking beauty of the ocean was better than any medicine that's out there. Thank you Kerri Mellert I love you...........

September 20, 2012

I'm really disappointed in the fact that it's so hard for people to understand the concept of being positive, just how much can be gained from this. I got flack that people will begin to think they brought the illnesses upon themselves. The point is NOT to look back but take life from this moment on and understand that you can affect your world with your thoughts and attitudes. We all have FELT the knot in our stomach when we're angry, probably broke into a cold sweat from fear, vomited from stress, what is this but thoughts and feelings affecting our bodies????????????????? It stands to reason maintaining a higher level of thought will produce a healthier body..............

September 23, 2012

Having a bad day, change places with these people. Wanna know what love is. Check out this mother. Feeling lost and helpless, put yourself in this mans place. Everyone has something to deal with, our unique road to travel. How we deal with it, whether it helps us grow or runs us into the ground, ,is up to us. It's a continuous on going process that can be lost in the "everyday". Mindfulness is a must. Make a promise to yourself to be mindful every day of you inner self and that you're not running strictly on the outer, material, ego based mind set...............

October 1, 2012

Today I am grateful for: the little corner in my bedroom where I can paint, do crafts, write my poems , lose myself in a project of some kind; the music stations on cable, so many choices for whatever your mood; my friend who framed my painting for me............

November 17, 2012

Today is the first day I've felt almost like myself in a very long time............... In what world do you go to the doctor with a booboo on your foot and end up being run through a blender? Oh, I forgot, cancer world...................................... I've learned one thing on this leg of the journey, "friends" who are only there when you're healthy, are not real friends. Sometimes you have to let go, but we all know that, we all have been in a situation where someone we thought would be there for us, let us down.

December 8, 2012

Memories- We all have a storehouse full of them. Many of them bring a smile to our face and we like to revisit them regularly. Some make us sad or angry and we find ourselves visiting them just as often. They have their place but dont spend so much time concentrating on your old memories that you forget to make new ones. Every second is an opportunity to make a special memory, it all depends on what you choose to do with it. Fill your storehouse with those wonderful moments that you live every day. Live in the now, don't compare to yesterday, don't try to recreate yesterday, today is where you are and what you have to work with. Draw it close, open all the doors of opportunity that this day offers and fill it with the wonders that life has to offer, for indeed every moment is filled with joys and wonders, be open to them, for the more you embrace them the more will come your way and you will find that you don't have to go to the memory bank to find happiness for today is filled with limitless opportunities............................

December 11, 2012

It's easy to get discouraged on the spiritual journey because the one thing you do not get is instant satisfaction. It's a process and most of us are working to replace many years of beliefs and thought patterns. I wish we could wake up in

the morning and have our whole way of thinking magically changed and in tune with spirit, but alas it is not so. I fall to the wayside as often as anyone else and sometimes it's a real fight to come back. These are the times when you need to go to an outer source, a workshop or seminar, a weekend retreat or just reading an inspiring book (or a paragraph or two every night before going to sleep) We're not alone in this and we should be grateful to those who have gone before us and paved the way, and most certainly we should take advantage of their knowledge. The important thing is to recognize that you have faltered and take the steps to get back on track.................................

December 20, 2014

We don't wake up at 3am and rush outside to force the sun to rise, nor are we out there at noon trying to force the moon to show up. We know, we have faith, that these events will take place when they are supposed to, without any help or interference from us. We need to develop that unfaltering faith when it comes to our life situations. Everything will come when it's supposed to, no matter what we do, or how much it may seem that our actions are hurrying things up they are not. All things come in their own time, everything has a season. We get frustrated and lose faith when our prayers are not answered when we want them to be, they will be, it's just not time yet. View life as a school and we must learn the lessons of one level before we can advance to the next. Ask yourself, what am I doing to thwart my advancement? What old beliefs do I need to let go of? Who or what have I not truly forgiven? Did I remember to be grateful? Am I doing my very best to overcome my ego self and live a spiritual existence? If your prayers are a long time in coming, inevitably the reason will be it just isn't "time". Stay in faith, continue your inner working and "know" as the sun will come up tomorrow so will my prayers be answered.....................

December 21, 2012

God helps those who help themselves, a phrase we have heard our whole lives, but what exactly does it mean? How are we supposed to help ourselves? The help we need to give ourselves in the work we do on the inside. Tuning in to the still small voice within. Learning to be in control of our thoughts and emotions, taking responsibility for our own actions. Accepting the fact that the victim mentality is a tool to feed the ego self and letting go of the past. I just had someone say "you don't know what I go through every day" no I don't, but I do know it's your choice to hold on to the hurt and horror. No one is standing over you compelling you to continue to revisit it. People don't want to hear "get over it" and that phrase is rather cold, but it's a reality. Until you get over yesterday, until you get over continuously go over and over hurtful events, until you learn that forgiving is not condoning you will be caught in the victim mentality. I gave in to my emotions and unfriended this person, I just don't want to try and help someone who doesn't want to be helped. My patting you on the shoulder and agreeing that all you have been through is horrible and letting you continue to wallow......is not helping. We all have the tool to make ourselves happier and better, when someone points it out that it's you and you refuse to use it, you're just not ready....................

December 22, 2012

I believe that a long time ago a man walked this earth who understood his relationship to his fellow man and the universe that created Him. I believe that he tried to make people understand theirs as well. I believe that there were others who came along either before or after him that had the same insight and tried to convey the same message in a different way. I believe that if you look, the base message in all "religions" is the same and if you strip away the bells and whistles and bastardization of man we are all being told the same thing. I believe it is up to each of us to do the work of finding the truth that is out there and begin to apply these principals to our individual lives, thus creating the ripple effect needed to bring us together as we were meant to be. I believe peace on earth can be achieved and hunger and homelessness and disease can be obliterated one person at a time.............

December 26, 2012

Well, here we are, another Christmas has been entered into the memory book and another new year is around the corner. We survived Y2K, 12/21/12 and numerous others predicted and feared events. We have also faced many unplanned and tragic events that have touched us all in some way. Will 13 be the magic tragic number???????? I'm surprised with so many people feeling the number 13 is unlucky that there aren't a slew of dire predictions out there for the coming year. My wish for this coming year is that we learn from our mistakes, not repeat the past, and learn to take responsibility for our actions, individually and collectively. I hope that people begin to understand that not taking things personally will eradicate so much negative in this world, and that our thoughts and words do indeed matter and make a to not let it fester, bless them, let them go and get on with the people who love you enough to sit with you when you're sick...........

December 27, 2012

Well, once again the best laid plans...........Our trip to YNH had to be postponed due to the storm that came through our area last night and today. I'm glad on one hand because they (Yale) have agreed to let me do the scans locally instead of doing a marathon of testing and seeing the doctor there all in one day. On the other hand, back to waiting .... again. I sure spend a lot of time waiting when I have a disease that they emphasize acting quickly is the best thing to do. Apparently those who advocate this have an unlimited supply of doctors and techs and equipment and can control weather and any other snafu that my show up. Sigh.........time for practicing the art of acceptance and faith that things are as they should be.

December 29, 2012

Look around you, right now where you are. Everything you see has one thing in common; do you know what it is? Everything started as an IDEA! Even the natural world started as an idea of the self aware creative consciousness of the universe. The power of the imagination is limitless and all we have to do is add the faith and emotions into the mix and we can create whatever we desire. We do it all the time without being aware of it, how empowering to be able to take control and realize we can and do make our own world by our thoughts and beliefs. Begin to take charge now and enjoy the ride as those things which we consciously wish to bring into our existence begin to manifest. Don't become discouraged, remember you have a lifetime of wrong thinking and misguided beliefs to replace and they will fight you at every turn. Stay steadfast on the path and reap the rewards....................

December 30, 2012

What is a family? A group of people who share the same blood line and then expand out to marriage partners and the new blood lines created there and so on and so on. Everyone has family members who are eccentric or hard to get along with or who say and do the wrong things at the wrong times, but the bottom line is, they are still family. We tolerate the eccentricities in our friends, we go out of our way to get along with the grumpy friend cause someone we love loves them, and we all have committed a faux pas or Freudian slip somewhere along the line, so why are the "family member" who fall into these categories left out? Family means everyone, the whole magilla, if not you're just part of a clique who pick and choose who they wish to include........................

Observations by Janine -2013

I am amazed at what barriers a person has to navigate when they embark on the cancer treatment journey. I've worked in the field for almost ten years now, however watching my brother and Shelli struggle to get treatment has been a significant eye opener for me.

When one has to leave their community to have access to sophisticated treatments, an army of helpers is required to make this work. No only does Shelli have to network with her friends for assistance; her daughter is called upon to take time from work to help with transportation.

I have grown to believe that when a health care provider announces the presence of cancer to a person, the individual begins to suffer an emotional loss, from that moment, of their life as they knew it. Essentially, the individual with cancer and their family becomes shrouded in a multitude of losses. The challenge is to unwrap that shroud and continue to live.

Elisabeth Kubler – Ross defined this grief process and identified five stages which individuals with terminal illness experience. I think companions, friends and family members of people diagnosed with cancer also experience a grief process. Together, though perhaps at different paces, they all navigate denial, anger, bargaining, depression and the end goal, acceptance.

There is also the financial burden that the person has to manage. There may be a loss of time from work, or loss of their job. Their family members may be called upon to help with transportation or access to food. The person may simply not be able to access treatment due to financial constraints.

My family and I have spent the past year, sort of sitting on the sidelines as Shelli endures the terrible side effects of the IL2 treatment. We help when we can, however what we are able to do seems so darn insignificant. I find the best way to cope is to continue with all the family traditions, meals and celebrations, events that can give Shelli a sense of normalcy.

Unfortunately, the tumors return. There are new ones on the left calf and more on the left foot. Her treatment team at MSK is very supportive. They urge cautious optimism, declaring that eventually the IL2 will overcome the ability of the cancer cells to replicate.

2013 brings along what seem like insurmountable challenges. There will be more treatments, entrance into the first clinical trial in February, more surgery and also melanoma tumors that will emerge on Shelli's scalp.

As I reflect on the conversations Shelli and I have had over the decades, I know that we've come to agree that our physical bodies have a beginning and an end. I struggle to stay positive. My limited experience with melanoma stage IV is that the all treatment is palliative and the outcome is death. I find myself returning more frequently to Michelle's "today I am grateful for l" page and also I continue to read her FB posts. In an odd sort of way, she is comforting me.

Posts

January 1, 2013

As I sit here and reflect on the past 12 months I'm awed at the incredible highs and lows that have been packed into them. I've lost old friends, and found some awesome new ones, I've made progress and had setbacks in my fight with cancer, I had an incredible cruise vacation with my daughter and a nightmare session with a cancer treatment. I made some steps forward and slipped back a few. I ended the year with a CT Scan to see if the treatment did any good, won't know till next week. I'm so grateful for the support of those who have stood by me and understand this disease may not be obvious but it takes its toll. I'm sad that there are some who I loved and depended on just don't have the gumption to "be there", and I'm over whelmed by the love and support of some of the new people in my life. I don't know what the future holds, none of us do, and as I try to hold on and stay in the positive place I send this sentiment out to all who stop by...... God Speed and Happy New Year!

My New Years Resolution: To be more like the sun. To continue to shine even if the clouds are surrounding me. To rise bright and shining every morning and not carry yesterday with me nor worry about tomorrow. To share my warmth and strength with everyone who crosses my path. To a light to everyone no matter where I am or they are. To be a source of comfort, and make people feel good as they seek me out. To work in harmony with the rest of nature to create the balance needed to keep us all going. Remember as you travel through your days, the sun is always shining, either behind the clouds or over the horizon, it's always there Our job is to know that and continue to live in its warm glow despite the appearance that it is not there.

January 5, 2013

Did you know that there is a place we all can go to find peace, joy, love, wealth or anything else we may desire and no one can keep us out or take away any of these things? Where? In our imaginations, what an awesome tool we have and we waste it. By now we all should at least have a slight clue that thoughts are things. When we go within and begin to imagine we are beginning the creative process, keep going add as much as you can, colors, smells, emotions, physical sensations BE WHAT YOU ARE IMAGINING and soon you will find it manifesting in the outer world. Totally understand this is the one place in the world that you have complete control, you choose what you say and do, what others say and do, what you have or don't have, how you look the whole magilla is right there and all you have to do is close you eyes and begin the process. Imagination is the predecessor to manifestation.................

January 11, 2013

Don't, for one nano second, believe that humans are the only intelligent life forms. BUT, if we are..........shame on us! If we truly are the only intelligent life form how can we rationalize destroying the only place fit for habitat? How do explain away the fact that all we do if try to destroy either our home or one another, in some way? Look at this picture, think about it, look how miniscule an area we take up. Then think about yourself as an individual in the scheme of things, not even a speck on the wall, and yet we think we're all that and a bag of chips. As long as we continue to function from the ego mindset we will destroy each other and/or the only place that is fit for us to live!! How can becoming spiritually aware affect this, well for one we would realize that the pursuit of money and things is not the way to go, we would realize that if we allow it, the Universe will and does supply us with everything we need. There would be no need for money, no need to run the rat race, no need to covet our neighbor's possessions, no need to steal or kill to get what or where we want, and that's just the beginning. Peace would reign because we would understand we are all one and we would treat our fellow man with love and respect. This is not a goal that will happen quickly, but if we don't start somewhere, and soon, it will be too late. Remember, it's our choice..........................

January 4, 2013

I do have one of these illnesses and it is the hardest thing in the world to see people you love and counted on fall to the wayside, because they just don't get that you're ill. You look find on the outside and ergo you are fine and if you don't feel like going out every time they call, it doesn't take long and they stop calling. They don't bother to stop in to see you, they are busy living their lives and the fact that you cannot keep up is your tough luck. There is also the problem if you are part of a support group for your ailment. People from your life before cancer become angry that you can go and hang out with your support group but not your other friends.   Because the people in the support group, understand and don't expect more from you then you can give, they are there no matter what because they know how important it is to you, they "get it" Most of us with these kind of illnesses do the best we can to live a normal life and not complain about our shortcomings, healthy people think you're lazy, bored, uninterested, or playing the pity me game when you can't go and do like they can. I just hope that all you healthy people out there never get any of these illnesses and if you do I hope your friends can see the reality of your situation...........................

January 6, 2013

Went for a brain MRI today, stopped in to see a friend in the hospital, went grocery shopping (all the motorized carts were taken so I walked around the store), by the time I got home.............in a hurtlocker with my foot and hip and exhausted. My daughter made me a cup of orange spice tea with honey, sitting there wallowing in the lovely smell and then sipping that heavenly combination was such a treat!!! I say it all the time, the little things in life, mean the most. The fact that someone made me a cup of tea and I could just sit back and totally get in that moment and enjoy every nuance of that cup of tea was priceless! Please, please, please, don't let those moments slip through you fingers................

January 14, 2013

Sometimes we are being nudged by spirit and no matter how hard we try we just don't understand. Theses are the times to just stop, stop trying to force anything and just back off. I cant tell you how many times I have wandered around the house feeling that I should be "doing something" but not having a clue as to what it might be. I wish I could say when I finally just stop that I have an epiphany and go on to a spectacular spiritual experience, but the truth is, it doesn't happen. Much of our journey is inner changes and I think sometimes that those times when you feel pushed but don't know why or where are the times when a huge inner change is taking place and somewhere down the road you will discover it. A specific direction will be obvious and you will know it when you feel it, uneasiness and feeling of being pushed and pulled is the resolution of an inner conflict that you're not even aware of. Learn to accept that uncomfortable feeling and stop trying to appease it with outer actions. Understand that there is inner work being done and it will show itself when the time is right.

January 15, 2013

Have my beliefs kept me from cancer? No, but they have made it possible for me to face each day and enjoy the many blessing that those days offer. Do they make me a saintly person who never gets angry or has a negative emotion? I wish! But they do give me the tools to overcome those emotions so I'm not living in the negative mode. Do I get discouraged? Does a bear poop in the woods? Have I forgiven all that I should? Every time I think I've mastered that, something comes up from deep within that I didn't even realize was there. The good news I have been given a way to allow these deeply buried negatives to surface so I can face them and let them go. Is this easy? Hell no! Is it worth it? I've been dealing with cancer for 2 1/2 years and managed to remain mostly calm and positive; I would consider that worth it. I have had positive results from the treatments I've taken and the disease has remained contained in one area of my body, need I say more? Have there been down sides? Unfortunately yes, some relationships have been totally severed, others will never be quite the same again. That makes me sad, but I understand that this journey is traveled by everyone at different speeds and some will take many side roads along the way. Am I a better person for all this? I am a perfect child of the Universe and what others think of me is tainted by their beliefs and where they are in their journey, so the question is moot. Have I been able to help others along the way? Only you can answer that because it is not I who do the work or reap the rewards for you. It's all up to you; I just give you something to think about. Do with it what you will ♥ ♥

January 16, 2013

Woke up to a blanket of snow today. So beautiful! I have so much respect for the peoples who lived in harmony with the natural order of things, like the Native Americans. They were so in tune with it and worked with it rather then against it. They weren't in a race to improve on what is, they just made the best of everything they were provided with and knew how to give back and keep the balance. I wish we had treated them better and learned from them instead of shoving onto barren land and telling them they were getting a good deal to be able to have a reservation at all! Their knowledge is slowly being lost as the younger generations are leaving the reservations (and who could blame them?) before they can learn all from the elders. Most of their knowledge is handed down by mouth and once all the elders are gone, so is the knowledge. We need to dig deep and find that connection with the earth again. We need to relearn how to live in harmony with her, respect her, nourish her and keep her alive so she continues to do the same for us...........................

January 17, 2013

What motivates people to do or not do things is a personal choice, made by their perceptions, beliefs and where they are. I hate when people keep things from me that I really should know, but, that's my perception of the situation so when someone keeps a "secret" and you find out about, don't be angry. We have a tendency to again, take things personally when we shouldn't. We may think it was wrong, not to be told, but I think it's more the ego screaming "you left "me" out, how dare you? We want the ego satisfaction of being asked to help, or provide something that we think only we can provide. Of course, there are situations where keeping secrets is covering up a potentially damaging situation i.e. you're cheating on your wife and those type of secrets need to be brought out into the open. Again, we need to examine the situation and not just react....................

January 20, 2013

You don't just wake up one morning a bitter, angry, unforgiving person. You build that person every time you dwell on the things you perceive to be wrong in your life. All the blame you place on others for your life being a mess blocks the flow of the Universal love like a dam on a river. Every time you revisit a perceived wrong, a hurt, go over an argument in your mind or let your anger take over you provide fodder to become exactly what you dislike in others! We will never be able to change others, the only thing we can change is ourselves. Do you like who you are? Are you happy? Do you feel loved and cared for? Do you understand that you are the only one who can change your life and the only way to change it is to change how you think about it and react to it? If you're not facing each day with expectations of wonderous things you are not living. If you stuck in the muck and mire of anger, guilt, regret, and all the other negative emotions you need to do a major house cleaning and start living the way we were meant to!!!

Other then some thyroid problems (which can be corrected with medication) still no adverse reactions to this new treatment. Having the doctors reiterate that visible results typically won't show up until after the 3rd treatment and then, not always, and if things are growing right now it doesn't necessarily mean I won't get results from this treatment, made me feel much better about everything. I'm confident once we get the thyroid meds adjusted properly that I will feel better. Till then I'm not going to obsess about being tired, I'll just nap when I need to (and be damn grateful that I can!) They also gave me some anti anxiety medication, which I have resisted for almost 3 years now. I guess it's time to give in, at least until I'm back on track. Ignoring outside help is not wise. I tried to do it all on my own, from within and I'm proud of the 3 years that I have succeeded, no shame in embracing all avenues of help. The Universe provides many avenues................................

February 2, 2013

Let's try this again............

I made my appointment with Sloan, they had all the paperwork ready for me to sign for the new clinical trial they are doing. The medicine in this trial is similar to the Yervoy I took first and tolerated well and had some response to, only this stuff seems to have a higher success rate and cause less liver problems. So apparently I'm in a clinical trail at Sloan. I wasn't ready for it to happen quite so rapidly, I saw the one doctor on Thursday, they called me Friday, I have an appointment with the surgeon on Monday plus and appointment to have the pretesting CT scan, back on the 14th for ECG and Xray then my first infusion is on the 21st! A little faster than I was ready for!!!!

I'm weary of all this, but as I look back I see that things fell in place for me to be where I am now. Before I didn't have people to take me to Sloan, now I do, we know that my body responded to a medication similar to this one and tolerated it well, so as intimidating and daunting this leg of the journey appears to be on one hand, on the other I'm right where I'm supposed to be....................

February 5, 2013

What an amazing day yesterday! It's blessing enough to find someone who is willing and able to take me to Manhattan, add to it another woman who is willing to give up her day and go along for additional moral support and you have an adventure. We arrived and left during what should have been peak traffic times. We ran into no problems with traffic either way. Sloan has a parking garage that offers shuttle service to the annex and the main hospital, we caught it all 3 times with the barest of minimum of waiting time or just as they were ready to leave but still had seats for us. The surgeon was able to remove the piece of tissue that has been giving me so much trouble and with stitches and cauterizing the remaining tumor we should have no more bleeding and a minimum of weeping. The procedure went well and was for all rights and purposes, painless.

I was able to get in a little early for the CT Scan so we did have to wait a bit but not the anticipated 5 or 6 hours. The tech was able to access the port so I didn't have to through having the IV in the arm scenario. So even though it was still a long and arduous day, it could have been so much more stressful! I am so grateful for all the small blessings that yesterday bestowed upon me. They made what could have been a horrible day a day of pleasant surprises and good news!!!! Just a reminder folks, always remember to see and appreciate the small blessings that every day brings us!

February 8, 2013

I have two amazing woman who are willing to make the trek to Manhattan and sit for God knows how long so I can take these treatments. I need more people so these awesome women are not stuck with the entire burden. I have sent an email to the American Cancer Society asking if they can help. I took a huge leap of faith in signing up for these treatments, not just trying to get there but putting myself out there as a guinea pig. Cancer is such a sneaky disease and causes so much more than physical symptoms. The tiredness that others cannot understand, the terrible emotional toll, many of us become different people and not always in a good way, no on understands because they cannot see what is going on. We struggle with pain, wondering what will become of us, will we be able to go into remission, and if so for how long and if not how long do we have to live. Hearing that so and so had cancer and beat it or is remission is meant to help, sometimes it does, more often then not it just shows that the speaker is ignorant of this disease, it's many idiosyncrasies and how personal it makes itself. Don't wait until someone near and dear to you is afflicted with this or some other disease. Make time to be with them, go out of your comfort zone and open your heart and mind to someone who is ill and possibly alone. Reach out to those who are the caregivers and offer to lighten their burden. You never know......

February 11, 2013

Struggling to get back in the grove these days. I had on nasty oozing bleeding hunk removed only to have another one start oozing. Having cancer is bad enough, having in your face cancer is a bit overwhelming some times. My discomfort level is increasing and my energy level is decreasing. Facing another unknown, after what I went through at Yale is, well let's just say, it's been a rough week. I needed to just withdraw for a bit, feel myself coming back albeit slowly. I refuse to let all my hard work go down the drain!!!! I know how much positive I have gotten and I know that it will continue to benefit me, just needed time to reconnect..........

February 12, 2013

I don't want pity, I need understanding, and I'm fighting for my life.

Can we truly make a difference? Of course we can! Again, what we contribute may not get us a Nobel Prize or any recognition from the masses at all, but if you take the time to reach out to one person, you have made a difference. One small act of kindness, one afternoon "sacrificed" visiting with someone instead of going to the mall or the movies or whatever else is "more fun" can lift the spirits of someone and give them that hands up that they may need. I can't tell you how much it meant to me to have a friend who has two extremely ill sons, take the time to pick out a Valentines Day card and buy a small box of candy and then deliver it. Of all people who have a legitimate reason NOT to find time she would be at the top of the list. We live in a world of fellow humans and we need the interaction. We were not designed as lone creatures, we are pack animals. There are those who can spend their lives in solitude but they are few and far between. I don't mind solitude, I enjoy my own company, and can always find something to do, but that doesn't mean an afternoon visit and a game of Scrabble are off the table. As always, we will reap what we sow. Examine your life, honestly, and peer into your future..............

February 15, 2013

One step at a time. Pre-testing finally done! Next step, first treatment next Thursday. I'd be lying if I said I'm not nervous, but I'm also optimistic. These therapies, as opposed to chemo, work on bolstering your own body's immune system to fight the cancer. I believe the body has its own ability to heal itself and have had minor results with the same type of treatment. I have learned so much about myself these past couple of years, and yes I have a whole lot more to learn and then learn to apply in everyday life but isn't that what this is all about anyway?

If you are not learning and growing everyday in some way, you need to reassess your life and your goals and aspirations. Take off the blinders of the physical ego driven world and enter the world of spirit. The Universe is there, just waiting for the invitation to come in...

February 22, 2014

It's been a little over 24 hours since the infusion. No side effects, minimal pain today, got good nights sleep Cause for celebration!!!! Still emotionally tired but hey who the hell cares, I can curl up and take a nap which is exactly what I'm going to do! I feel so much better, like a shift in the force has taken place in a good way. Never underestimate the power of the Universe or the role you play in it ♥ ♥ ♥ ♥

March 3, 2013

I've seen it first hand. The Universe steps in at the 11th hour and prayers are answered and life takes a dramatic turn for the better. What I have noticed is, these 11th hour redemptions come when we finally give in, give up and stop trying to manipulate what, how, when and where. Like the alcoholic who has to hit bottom before he/she can really change, many of us have to experience the total surrender of our egos desires in order to have them fulfilled. Thy will be done, doesn't mean resignation, it means acceptance, understanding that we in our human form, with all our human limitations cannot know what is truly in our best overall interest. It means trusting that there is only one force, and it is a loving, caring, formidable force dedicated to giving you the best of everything. Sometimes it means just sitting and doing nothing when the world around you is going crazy. It means understanding that what may appear to be "bad" is indeed a good thing and part of our overall individual plan in this leg of our journey. When things are the worst, when it's the hardest, is when it's most important to dig deep, find that seed of faith and "Let go and let God"...

March 4, 2013

Choices, they are always there, but not always easy to make. I've been having a bleeding problem with a large tumor on my leg. It can be removed, but I will have to deal with an open wound, perhaps forever. Or I can be really, really, really careful and try to keep it from bleeding and wait to see if the treatment will shrink the sucker and then I won't have to deal with any wound. I'm not that active as it is, discomfort, pain, not having properly fitting footwear make it really difficult to get around and really do anything, now it will be even less activity. I really want to wait and see if the treatment will work, but on the other hand I don't want to have to deal with a badly bleeding lesion. Sigh.......

March 5, 2013

Have you fluffed your chakras today? We have no problem accepting as fact that there are organs within our bodies that run certain functions of the body as a whole but readily poo poo the idea of energy centers that need attention as well. The smallest particle we have discovered is the atom which is composed of energy and air, what magical leap does it take to understand that we are in fact large masses of energy and something is keeping it all in control, doing what it's supposed to? Take a few moments and learn something about your chakras and then learn to listen to them. They exist and are another tool we have been given to access that which we cannot see.............

March 11, 2013

We all know how detrimental it is to swim against the current and how exhausting it is, but even going with the flow can take its' toll sometimes. There are times when just treading water or floating along is necessary. We need to recognize these times not as failures but as recharging or refueling if you will. As long as you don't slip into thinking you have to start swimming against the current because right now you're getting nowhere, you're ok. Spirit is always working and nothing you do to make your spiritual journey better is ever wasted. Sometimes it may mean, just floating along for a while. We need to be mindful of these times and not try to rush things. It's like having a pot of water on the stove; it will boil when it's ready and nothing we do can make it any different. If we have done all that is required from a physical level, we may find ourselves treading water until God's time catches up with ego time. Learn to enjoy these times, take advantage of them, lie back and enjoy the anticipation of reaping the harvest of what you have sown............

March 13, 2013

No matter what is happening in your personal existence, never lose the ability to be truly happy for the good news of someone else. A positive upswing for my friend from the Kansas Animal Shelter gives my heart a lift and puts a smile on my face. I know how hard this man is struggling to make sure these animals are cared for and I know the sacrifices he has made. Any small victory is a major triumph and I relish in the good news. Good news about a friend, a visit from a friend this afternoon (♥ Reenie) all is right with the world.

March 17, 2013

Those of you who read my posts are familiar with my take on positive thinking and that we can and do create our own realities. There is something out there called The Hundred Monkey theory. There was a study of a monkey troop in Japan. One of the monkeys began washing his sweet potato in the salt water in a certain way. Before long the whole troop was following suit. The kicker is, a troop of monkeys 100 miles away who had no physical contact with the original group began doing the same thing!!! The hundred monkey is the scientists symbol for when a critical mass within a species is reached. Once that critical mass is reached the entire species begins to think/act in the same way. If enough people think and act that we will be annihilated by nuclear war, it will happen. If enough think and believe it's impossible we can indeed avoid the destruction. We have to ability to "change" the collective consciousness, to make this a better world. I know how difficult it is to look beyond what you senses tell you. But that's what faith is. And if you have ever done any reading or watched any programs related to your senses and how reliable they are you know that they are indeed deceptive little devils. We are our brothers keeper weather we know it or not. Hopefully by being aware of our contribution to the whole enough of us will change our thoughts and beliefs and we will see this world become a better place.................

April 2, 2013

Sometimes we just have to have faith that support will sustain us until we arrive at our destination. It sure gets scary and we have to keep our attention on the destination and keep walking the path without looking down or letting go. You may reach a stretch that seems impossible to cross without falling into the abyss. Take that step (leap) of faith and continue onward. Standing there swaying in the wind will just reinforce your fear and doubt, find you pace and push on. It's ok to stop and regroup now and again; it's not okay to become stagnant! I read somewhere that the further along the path you traverse the less signs your receive, the more you must depend upon the inner faith and strength you have fought so hard to develop. The old adage, it's always darkest before the dawn is a truism. The hours before sunrise are truly the darkest. Know in your heart of hearts the sun lies just under the horizon and will indeed slowly begin to shed its light until once again you are surrounded by the light............................

April 4, 2013

Other than some thyroid problems (which can be corrected with medication) still no adverse reactions to this new treatment. Having the doctors reiterate that visible results typically won't show up until after the 3rd treatment and then ,not always, and if things are growing right now it doesn't necessarily mean I won't get results from this treatment, made me feel much better about everything. I'm confident once we get the thyroid meds adjusted properly that I will feel better. Till then I'm not going to obsess about being tired, I'll just nap when I need to (and be damn grateful that I can!) They also gave me some anti anxiety medication, which I have resisted for almost 3 years now. I guess it's time to give in, at least until I'm back on track. Ignoring outside help is not wise. I tried to do it all on my own, from within and I'm proud of the 3 years that I have succeeded, no shame in embracing all avenues of help. The Universe provides many

avenues..............................

April 5, 2013

Inner peace comes when you realize that the decision to embark on

the spiritual path has no defined destination. It's a constant unfolding of

inner communication and understanding of who and what we truly are in

relationship to this world and the universe. It is a continuous unfolding of

inner awareness, learning what unconditional love truly is and how to

apply to every living creature. It is coming to an understanding that our

physical bodies are not who or what we are and the world we think of as

solid and real, is in fact a constant exchange of energy which we create and

manipulate with thought and emotion. It is the art of truly letting go of

everything we perceive to be real and allowing the Universal truth to

manifest itself.

May 1, 2013

Wonderful at times, extremely scary at times, confusing, daunting,

frustrating, and downright painful. Many who start the journey will fall to

the wayside; others will reach a certain level and become stagnant. A few,

who have the tenacity to continue will come to the realization that the goal is the journey itself and will continue. Whatever your choice, it's yours to make..........................

July 27, 2013

I just realized something.............the way the amputation was done, above the knee; I don't have a lap any more. Let us take a moment to pay homage to the lowly lap. I held my baby girl on my lap and rocked her to sleep, read her books, sang songs and pulled her in close when illness befell. I've held literally hundreds of plates of awesome (and not so awesome) picnic foods and plates provided by a heartbroken survivor as we gathered to remember; I cannot count the number of dogs, cats, and other small critters I have had curled up on my lap, (I still haven't figured out who was consoling who, or which one of us was enjoying the cuddle time more). The lap was a total convenience on those rare occasions that we went to a restaurant that actually provided cloth napkins you could put on your lap, it has proved to be a wonderful holder, carrier, balancer of a slew of articles over the years, my lap top has now become a one thigh top and any little people in my life will have to settle for sitting on a half a lap if they are so motivated. Take a moment, sit down, and appreciate the unnoticed, unappreciated, but wonderful little space we so casually call a lap......................

August 22, 2013

I had two people tell me today how much they admire me and what a special person I am. The truth is I am no different than any one of you out there. The below says it all. We all have it. The difference is I chose different thought patterns, attitudes, reactions, and I try very hard to keep my emotions from taking over, without repressing them or denying them. Life situations can make you feel like your living in a blender being whipped round and round with no control and no way out. There are things that are going to happen that we just cannot change, what we can change is how we think about it, react to it, let it effect us. This new tumor is very close to my face and I feel new bumps even closer and if you don't think that freaks me out, well, I don't know what to say. I'm concentrating on finding that sweet place that knows "it's all good". I will let the doctors take care of the outside and I will take care of the inside. I'm seeing myself cancer free and walking with my prosthetic and getting out there and enjoying life and also making sure I physically do something to make this a better world. Maybe I will work in the soup kitchen with Victoria L., maybe I will volunteer at the hospital, but I definitely will put my money where my mouth has been this last 3 years. Don't put me on a pedestal, dig within yourself and find that same divine essence that we all have, and begin to enjoy the freedom from fear, worry, unforgiving and all the other

negatives we so readily allow into our life situations..................................

August 29, 2013

When to student is ready the teacher will appear, don't rush into

anything when the time is right it will happen. These and a dozen other

similar idioms (for lack of a better word) were never truer than they were

today. I have been absolutely anti-chemotherapy from day on (which for

you newbies was 3 years ago). I have reached the point where, right now, it

is the only choice I have right now. The new tumors have disqualified me

from the trial and there are no new ones open right now. It had been

mentioned to me before and I expected to be a serious mess today,

but............something inside of me must have done it's magic and I was

open to this, did not fall apart, actually asked a few intelligent questions

and feel that "it's all in the timing". They have had a 20-30% success rate

doing the chemo as a follow up to this treatment for those of us who have

not responded positively to the treatment. That's better odds then a lot of

the other stuff I've tried and they will administer it over 3 days to minimize

the side effects. It can be done locally, so I won't have the stress of trying

to get rides to NYC for at least 9 weeks, and I can do the follow up CT

scan locally as well because it's no longer attached to the trial. As for the

itching............would you believe Benadryl?????????? It never occurred to me. If it doesn't work they have other stuff but they recommend the Benadryl first. It's all good...

August 26, 2013

Working in spirit requires sacrifice. Something none of us want to hear or for that matter do. I'm just as guilty as the next guy. I have been told on several occasions that sugar feeds cancer, but did I give it up. Nope! Now I have more to deal with. As much as we fight it, if we're honest with ourselves we will realize that the things we are unwilling to give up or sacrifice are merely things of the physical world. Sweets had become a substitute for so many things in my life for so long that I lost the thread. I was thinking correctly, doing affirmations, learning to control my emotions, and all the while I was feeding the ego self, literally and figuratively. An extremely hard pill to swallow, but part of the process is to be honest with yourself. (There are those feet of clay again). So, I say to you find those ego fed bumps in the road and get rid of them. We have to look deep and hard sometimes to find these areas of sacrifice that are needed for our advancement but look we must or we will indeed stagnate, or situations will worsen...............................

August 29, 2013

Of all the wonderful, uplifting, positive sayings I've seen, this has to be my favorite! Have you ever put someone's kind act in the realm of answered prayer? Probably not, we tend to want fireworks and bands in answer to our prayers and overlook the answers that come in the packaging of another human being. What better representation of the Universe than one of its children reaching out to you, no matter how small. The smile from a stranger that you responded to and felt a moment of happiness, the door that was held open for you, the pleases and thank yous, the person who give up their place in line for you. Granted they are not the new job you want or the healing or the things that you're consciously praying for, but you inner self is constantly in touch with the Universe telling it, I need to feel happy, I need to know that this world is not filled with just evil, greedy, self-absorbed people. I need to know you are here. So the next time a stranger smiles at you take a moment to say "Thank you God, I needed that"

August 31, 2013

There is a book called "The Secret Garden" and I will admit I have never read but from what I understand it's about a little girl who has this secret garden that only she knows about (hence the term secret lol). Do you know we all have our own personal secret garden? It's our subconscious and it's seeded with all our thoughts and depending on how we tend to it we will either have a beautiful flourishing garden filled with all the flowers we want, or it will be filled with weeds, nettles, burdock and all the other not so pretty and nice things found in the outdoors. The flowers represent the good, uplifting, loving, abundant things in life, and obviously the weeds and such represent all the troubles and woes we find in our life. If you knew that every time you reacted to someone else with anger, bitterness, hatred or any other negative that you were feeding the weeds in your garden and making negative experiences in your life would you still allow yourself to do that? Or, would you take a moment and take a deep breath and react with kindness and love, no matter how the other person is acting? Doing so feeds the flowers in your garden and will bring forth nothing but good in your life. It takes practice, self disipline, awareness and time, but so does having a real physical garden and that , although they do bring pleasure to the senses, will not change your life situation. Tending to your own "seceret garden" will in time turn you entire life experience around.......

August 31, 2013

Having only one leg and trying to use a walker when you're doubled

over with gas pains, just doesn't work, cause eventually your

forehead is against the walker and you're doing the hokey pokey ;(

Sept 3, 2013

THIS IS THE FIRST TIME SINCE I'VE OPENED THIS PAGE THAT I
HAVE DONE THIS. I NOTICE THAT OUR MEMBERSHIP IS AT 390,
I WOULD TRULY LOVE TO SEE THIS NUMBER HIT 400. IF YOU
KNOW ANYONE WHO YOU THINK MIGHT ENJOY THIS PAGE,
BENEFIT FROM IT AND/OR CONTRIBUTE TO IT PLEASE ASK
THEM IF THEY WOULD LIKE TO JOIN OUR LITTLE FAMILY.
LET'S SPREAD THE WORD THAT GRATITUDE OF THE SMALL
THINGS IN LIFE BEGETS THE BIGGER
THINGS................................THANK YOU ADVANCE THOSE OF
YOU WHO PARTICIPATE. LOVE, PEACE, HEALTH AND JOY TO
ALL OF YOU.

If you lost you cell phone, would you cease to exist? If the word

mother or father were suddenly obliterated from the language would you

turn into a pile of ashes? If there were no longer any political parties would

you burst into flames? Of course not, you would still be you. All those

labels are meaningless and until we can let go of them we will be forever

mired down in the muck of the ego world, a servant to it instead of its

master. We are so indoctrinated into those labels as identifying who we are

we lose our true selves. In truth all the things we truly are, are the words

86

that have no physical definition. I am love, I am forgiveness, I am kindness, gratefulness, compassion, joy, peace, well you get the idea. These are the words we should be using to identify ourselves. The next time some one pisses you off, say to yourself, "I am forgiveness." or "I am perfect understanding." and see how your whole being reacts. Practicing these ideas will bring manifestation into your world. And it works with finances also. If you're constantly saying "I'm broke," I don't have enough money" you will continue to find lack if you affirm "I am opulence." it will come into your world. When it comes down to the nitty gritty, our only job here is to believe and act upon those beliefs. If you say I am love, but act unloving you are showing disbelief. Say it, act it, see it come into manifestation ....

September 3, 2013

I truly believe the word **CAN"T** needs to be globally stricken from the vocabulary! Can't is a cop out word, a substitute for I won't, I don't want to, that will take more effort than I'm willing to expend. There are things we are unable to do, and the difference is when someone says I'm unable to do that, you can ask why and there has to be a reason. Right now I'm unable to walk without help. Why? Because I only have one leg and I haven't got the strength to walk/hop without the help of a walker. When someone says, "I can't." and you ask them why 99 3/4 percent of the time the answer is "I just can't!" Come one folks be honest with yourself, you don't want to or your just not willing to try. Think about it, what are you limiting you life by with the words I can't. Are you truly unable or just unwilling? Something to think about.................................

September 4, 2013

I give myself permission to be sad, have lost 2 people who I cared for deeply in the past couple of days................. I lost a dear friend, one of my first face book buddies, and the hole that is left is just as deep as one left by a friend I see every day. I will miss her ....

September 6, 2013

Took my first spill today.............What a trip, trying to figure out how to get up. Finally scooted across the floor on my butt to the stairs and managed heft myself up high enough to get my leg under me and get back in my chair (Thank God for Physical Therapy!). Almost as funny as the doctor trying to "help" me get on the scale yesterday. It's a traditional balance scale, and there was not really anything to hold onto. Here's the doctor grabbing my leg to help me hop onto it. I swear I don't know how we did it but I got up on the damn thing. I will begin by chemo either next week or the week after, it has to be administered over three days and they prefer to do it in the beginning of the week, in case there are any complications. I have another doctor's appointment on Monday so they will either do Tues, Wed., Thur of next week or wait till the week after and do Mon., Tues., and Wed., waiting for the phone call. I think I'm going to go back to bed and lick my wounds. All I can say is, I'm grateful I didn't hit my head where that tumor is, that I didn't seriously hurt myself, and that I was able to get up with a minimum of trauma. :

September 8, 2013

Being surrounded by those you love has a tremendous healing power. Just the presence of people who love you creates a circle of love and healing. This alone can do miracles, add the power of prayer and you have an unbeatable power. Sometimes, when we're not feeling well, we turn away those who love us and want to be near, perhaps we should rethink this practice and allow loved ones and their unspoken love do its' magic. There is noting worse then lying in a bed, feeling the worst you've ever felt and having someone turn people away. The excuse is, they need their rest. I know from experience, just the presence of someone you love works wonders. As sick as I was during one of my treatments, I know that all the countless hours my daughter spent, just sitting there, made things better. When they put me in ICU, alone and sicker than I ever thought a human being could be and survive, when they finally let her in things changed. We don't have to talk, just be there. Hold you're loved ones hand or just sit there with your hand on their arm or leg; allow the energy of your love to flow into the patient. Many wondrous things can and will happen.

September 9, 2013

ser·en·dip·i·ty (srn-dp-t)

n. pl. ser·en·dip·i·ties

1. The faculty of making fortunate discoveries by accident.

2. The fact or occurrence of such discoveries.

3. An instance of making such a discovery.

I have always thought that was such a cool word and wanted to be able to use it in my life. I believe today is the day. I made and appointment with a neurologist to possibly address to phantom pain issues) that I had to cancel and reschedule for today, which happens to be the same day I had the appointment with the person who will be making my prosthetic. I was going to cancel the neurologist appointment, but my daughter said "Why not wait and see how it goes with the prosthetic guy first?" , so I didn't cancel the appointment. While at the prosthetisis (?) office he mentioned that he wanted me to see this certain doctor to write a script for the leg. (I had one but for red tape reasons he needed one that was more detailed) The doctor he wanted me to see.................was the neurologist I had the appointment with! So I didn't have to wait another couple of weeks for the doctor's appointment to get the script I needed. How cool is that? This makes me feel better about the chemo. Why, you ask. Because if the Universe is working out the wrinkles in getting my leg, it plans on me being around to use it!!!!! Be mindful of how things are unfolding around you, you may be surprised with a serendipitous moment of your own...........

September 10, 2013

.... Been difficult to come here lately, my left eye is swollen and I thought I had a sinus infection. The doctor says it's from the cancer............ I do have a couple of bumps by my ear and very close to the hairline on that side. Processing this and the fact that after 3 years of fighting it, chemo is now my only option has me a little off base these days. I feel like Job and am working very hard at not giving in to all the negatives connected with what's going on in the physical plane. To bad they can't cut my head off like they did my leg

September 11, 2013

Eye tired and puffy, need to let it rest, gonna lay down and listen to TV for a while. Nite all, sleep in peace, wake in joy, and live in faith.........

September 12, 2013

Thought patterns like just about everything else we do, are habits. Something happens; we react to it, form a thought about it and impress it on our consciousness. The next time something even vaguely similar happens we pull from our "experience" and apply the same thought pattern to it, eventually the subconscious grabs hold of it sends the super conscious the message that this is what we want and voila what was once a passing thought has now become a destructive thought pattern. The good news is, just like any other habit, you thinking patterns can be changed. And, just as any other habit, it isn't easy, it takes commitment and being kind and forgiving to yourself if you "fall off the wagon" so to speak.

Not a morning person? Would you like to start the day out happy and full of energy? Well, do it. First thing when you open your eyes, thank the Universe for another glorious day. Put a smile on your face, (and I know how hard that is at zero dark thirty in the morning) and swing you legs over the bed and hit the floor with a song in your heart and a smile on your face. It isn't going to happen overnight, breaking any habit takes time, but stick with it and you will reap the rewards. Pick a thought pattern you would like to change and work on that one thing, then the concept of a complete overhaul isn't so intimidating. Once you see that it does indeed work, pick something else. As I've said before, it's a journey and the destination is not the goal but the little successes along the way. What thinking habit will you pick?...............

Today I am grateful for: The man who's making my prosthetic actually coming to my house to bring the correct size shrinker and some other apparatus the name of which I cannot remember; finally after more than an hour of trying I managed to get that new apparatus on correctly (at least I think so) ; finally having all the meds I need to begin my chemo next week....

September 13, 2013

My day consisted of getting up, having breakfast, doing physical therapy, having my hair washed, trying to put the new apparatus on my leg correctly and a nap. I woke up in time to make dinner, ate, watched some TV and I'm pooped!! No words of wisdom here today, just a tired body and an inner struggle to keep in the faith with the prospect of chemo hanging over my heard.......

September 14, 2013

Today I am grateful for: living in such a beautiful place surrounded by so many of God's precious creatures (the picture below was taken a few moments ago in my driveway); to whoever suggested vinegar and water for the itching, it seems to be helping; dirt/soil without it nothing would grow, there would be no mud puddles for children to splash in, no mud pies, nothing to absorb the rain or provide burrows for many small critters to hunker down in over the winter, no place to bury or dead and no reason for mothers tell their children not to get dirty.................................

September 15, 2013

This if just an fyi to those of you who follow my posts. As you know I'm notorious for typos and bad spelling, with the swelling in my eye expect things to be a bit more chaotic. I do reread them, but as I am the worlds worst proof reader and see what is supposed to be there I don't catch the boo boos until it's too late to edit. So to all the English majors out there..................sorry bout that.

September 16, 2013

Today I am grateful for: a lovely visit from my niece Dorothy , 3 check in phone calls from friends; making to the night before the chemo starts without having a major meltdow (a few minor ones but nothing earth

shattering................................

As much as the idea of chemo scares me, the amount of things going on in my head and face scares me more. I have put myself in the hands of the Universe from day one, trusting it would see me though this. I don't know where it's taking me and even though there is a goodly amount of fear going into this part of me is looking forward to it because I know it's all good. Whatever the outcome of this journey is I can't say I haven't gotten anything out of it, and I hope I have given something back. I don't know how much else there is to learn or by what medium but I'm firm in my conviction that it's all good. I may not be here for a while, depends on how I tolerate the chemo, so if I'm not up to posting please continue to be kind to one another, to love one another, to reach out to one another, to be grateful for all the big and little things that life offers and most of all know in your heart of heart that we all are indeed one, part of the whole, a piece of the Divine just by the fact that we exist............

September 22, 2013

CHEMO SHELLI STYLE:

First of all they pump you full of as much fluid as humanly possible and then they give you a diuretic! In order to keep track of your

95

kidney function, they have to measure your output, so they give you this lovely little plastic dohickey they call a "hat" that goes between the toilet and the seat. Ok, not so bad, except the first time I missed it completely, the second time it was more or less half and half and the third time it fell in the potty. New plan, move hat back to front of potty and move body till we have contact. This ended up with me hanging on the very very teeniest edge of the potty possible without falling flat on my face, but we got our measurements so it was all good. Then, my friend who had come to sit with me decided she would help and put the "hat" on for me...............you know that feeling when your body tells you that should be connecting with something solid and you're not?????? Try getting out of that with one leg, hanging on to a bar 1/4 inch from the edge of the potty. Thank God for physical therapy, I didn't fall in. Then, they had to weigh me to make sure I was getting the proper amount of medicine. They have a regular doctor's balance scale that is just a bit to high for me to hop on. I'm sitting looking down the hallway watching my doctor and nurse trying to build a ramp with pieces of a cardboard box and a bunch of books, all different shapes and OMG!!!! I went down the hall and looked around and asked the nurse if the scale moved, it did, I said "There's bars in the bathroom aren't there? Why not move the scale in there and I'll pull myself up on it." Problem solved. Joke of the day - "How many medical professionals does it take to weigh a one legged woman?" "NONE"

So far I have come through amazingly well. A lot of edema in my left eye, my eyebrow and cheekbone were touching, a teeny bit of woopsie in the tummy but nothing serious at all. Very - very tired. I've been sleeping more than anything, but hey, I'll take it. The eye is still a bit swollen and it's hard for me to see to well but I wanted to let everyone know I'm doing fine and thank you for your love and support.

September 23, 2013

So many of us go through our lives searching for signs, praying for a personal miracle to assure us that there is indeed a higher power and it does care for us and will help us, that we miss the everyday guarantees that surround us. In our everyday lives we make friends, marry, have dozens of relationships and I have never once heard someone say, "You can only be my friend if you do such and such or act in a certain way?" Do you stop loving someone because they bring you carnations instead of roses?

We are surrounded by the hand of God every moment of every day, but we ignore it because it isn't coming in the packaging we want. When something is offered in love over and over again and is consistently rejected, why would you think that something else, better, would be offered? We must learn to see and acknowledge the hand of God that is given us every day in order to receive more. If you ask for God to speak to you and ignore the song of the meadowlark you are ignoring His voice. When you pray for Him to reach out and touch you and yet not feel the warm breeze against your face you are turning away from Him. Open your eyes, your heart, your mind, let spirit take over and connect you with your life source. We are so much more then these physical bodies we inhabit at the moment. Ask and you will receive, seek and you will find, knock and the door will be opened unto you......................

October 2, 2013

Took my first "walk" today across the living room and back a couple of times. Weirdest feeling EVER!!!! You kinda have to kick the foot forward and have it land on the heel, then tighten up the butt muscle to lock the knee apparatus so you don't go flying and then put your weight on that "leg" to bring the real foot forward. All I can say is I'm going to have the tightest butt muscles in town by the time I learn to use this thing, It (the prosthetic) is quite heavy and of course awkward, it's all just going to take time, getting used to and lots o practice!   I had no idea what was involved in the life of an amputee and believe me folks it not cut and dried by any means. You have to deal with body changes, ie gaining or losing weight, and that doesn't necessarily mean all over, your stump can change size according to you activity. There are blisters and sores and what you can and can't do. I don't know if my "leg" will allow me to kneel which I wanted to be able to do so I could garden next year. I will have to talk to the prosthetic guy about kneeling. It's like getting a full set of dentures and having to keep tweaking them all the time instead of just having to have them tweaked until they fit right and then you can go on. I have no idea what the Universe has in store for me but it must be awesome because it certainly has put me through my paces this last few years and now that things a beginning to look up I'm curious to see what will come next. No one can ever tell me that prayer and positive thinking and attitude don't help. I'm living proof that they do...............

October 6 2013

As we traverse through this physical journey we must always be mindful that we share this experience with not only other humans, but plants and animals as well. If we leave out caring for this planet and all she has to offer, we are not doing our "job". We were given such a beautiful gift to enjoy, and every creation here contributes to our growth in some way. We are so stuck on the physical that we are destroying our planet, allowing plants and animals to disappear, abusing animals, destroying our waters, the list goes on and on. Who will care for this planet if we don't? Imagine how you would feel if you gave you child a gift of such beauty and diversity just to see it abused and destroyed.

How can we honestly call ourselves children of God and then turn around and abuse and destroy all that has been given us? Each of us must do our part to ensure that our world and everything in it continues to thrive. Even the smallest effort will make a difference, be mindful of what you are doing on a daily basis that either helps our world or is eating away at it. We don't know what the Universe had in mind for these features of our world but I honestly believe that every plant and animal has a specific purpose for us and a path of it's own in the scheme of things. Let us stop being so arrogant in thinking we are above them because we are "human". Be thankful for the beauty of it all and care for it as if you're life depended on it - for it just might...

October 7, 2013

Laughter, what a wonderful thing. I love to laugh, love to make people laugh, love having laughter in my life. I have no problem making an ass out of myself if it makes someone laugh. Leaving the oncologists office today I had a great opportunity that I just couldn't pass up. The height of the receptionist desk is just about eye level for me in my wheel chair. Hit by a scathingly brilliant idea, I lifted my head up so my nose was laying on the counter. The girl was looking at her puter and when she looked up I just said "Kilroy was here". Now I'm pretty sure she's way to young to know who Kilroy was so it just must have been a totally ridiculous sight cause she just lost it. I left my chemo session giggling and feeling great.

Never take yourself or life situations to seriously to the point where you can't laugh. Laughter is healing, something happens physically when you laugh and you just feel better all around. Learn to laugh at yourself, find the humor in every situation (yes even the inappropriate ones, for those are the times laughter is needed most, just be mindful not to offend others and know who you can share those inappropriate giggles with). Throw your head back and bring that wonderful guffaw right from your toes. The Universe loves the sounds of music and laughter........

October 12, 2013

Is it truly possible to "reinvent" ourselves? Of course it is. It is about the only possibility we actually can achieve and control. Once you understand and begin to practice changing your thinking and attitudes you're on the way to creating the person you should be. How do we learn not to take things personally? Remember that whatever the other person is reacting to is the circumstance and it wouldn't matter who was standing there at the moment, that person would react the same way to that set of circumstances, so it has not one thing to do with you personally. Shrug it off, understand that it is the other person's problem and really has nothing to do with you. We are not responsible for any one else but ourselves and once we accept that responsibility we will find peace. Stop blaming other people, circumstances, the past, the unknown future, take control of who and what you are and what you want your life to be. It isn't easy and there will always be times when you fall back into the old pattern, but recognize it, and then let it go. How freeing it is to know that no person or circumstance can shake you unless you allow it. If we spent 1/4 of the time working on ourselves as we do trying to mold the physical world to our specifications this would be a much happier, cleaner, and more peaceful, more loving world to live in.................

October 16th 2013

Sometimes life situations are so overwhelming that the thought of having anything to be thankful for is far beyond your capabilities. Those are the times when you need to just say "Thank You", and leave it at that. The simple act of saying those words sets up a positive vibration in your world. You don't have to specify anything, just put yourself in a state of gratitude and the universe will respond. The added bonus is when you're saying thank you, you're not focusing on all the negative going on around you, you're letting it go if only for a few moments and you will find peace in that moment. Make it a mantra for a few moments every day, thank you, thank you, thank you, simple, easy, and so very very powerful. Start small but start. Take control of your thoughts, emotions, and life situations with that small act of gratitude..................

October 24, 2013

Sitting here with Henrietta and Stumpy getting to know each other. Looking over the past 40 months and all the changes that have taken place. Other than the obvious the internal changes are monumental. Oh I still have buttons that can be pushed, but now I'm aware of it and most of the time can catch myself before I react. When I do react it's over with, I don't cling to it and make myself angry and hurt over a trivial incident. I'm amazed at the people who have come into my life and how positive and inspiring they are. I sit outside with the wind blowing and close my eyes and soar with the wind, I try to keep my scented candles going as much as possible. They bring such a warm and homey feeling to my surroundings. I know how powerful visualization is and spend time each day doing visualization exercises for my health and being able to walk comfortably and easily with Henrietta. I realize that all this takes time, and time is something most people will say they don't have. The greatest gift we can give is the gift of time, and who deserves your time more than you do? If someone came to you and said "I have a magic potion that can change your life for the better, with no side effects and no negative repercussions." wouldn't you be willing to try it. Well there is a magic potion out there and its called time. The best part, we all have access to it, it's free and it works. Don't let the woes of the physical ego driven outer rob you of the precious gift of time.

November 4, 2013

I find myself a tad off balance these days. When the simplest of tasks becomes a major undertaking, not getting sucked into the world of the physical to the point where it rules your thoughts and emotions is to say the least a daunting task. I sit here at my computer, wearing Henrietta feeling everything from actual pain to just a tingling like it's been asleep and is now waking up is just plain freaky! It's made of plastic and metal, it cannot feel, and yet there they are mocking me. The simple task of making the bed, or going to the bathroom are major, time consuming feats. I have to dig deep and remind myself to be grateful for all that I do have and can do, even if it is different then what I'm used to, I can still do most of it.

These are the times when we really have to rely on our inner spirit to pull us through. The ego self is pulling at you, trying to get you to give in and give up. Just think about how hard this is, how you can't get yourself a cup because the shelf is just too high, how long and difficult a trip to the bathroom is. Don't you wish things were like they used to be, remember how easy it was to make your bed, you could just get up and walk to the bathroom, you should feel sorry for yourself, here let me show you all you're missing and how much better it was before. Sound familiar?

This is the dialogue of the ego self, trying it's hardest to take control again and suck you back into its world. And, as I've always preached, your thoughts are in your control, no one else. The thoughts of the ego self and the higher consciousness thoughts of spirit are both under your control. Just because I know this, does not mean I don't struggle with it as much as anyone else. Being so tired all the time makes it even more difficult because it does take strength and the ability to focus to work on changing your thoughts. So as I continue to teeter as this poor seagull, I know I will prevail and summon the strength and faith to overcome this epic battle....

November 8, 2013

Sometimes we have to take positive thinking to the next step and try positive doing. We all have days when we wake up and just feel down before our feet even hit the floor. (I personally think a lot of it has to do with what goes on in our minds during the sleep process. I have woke up crying from dreams that I don't really remember, or remember so vividly they could ruin my whole day) My point is, there will be times when the negative comes from a place we cannot identify so we're not really sure what thoughts we should pick to make us feel better, or the ones we're trying just don't seem to be working.   These are the times when you should reach down and grab those boot straps and do something positive. Something that makes you feel good, holds your attention, brings you peace or happy memories, or anticipation of bringing happiness to someone else. I like to bake on those kinds of days. There is something so comforting and homey about putzing around the kitchen and creating something decadent to enjoy with your family. Not a baker? That's okay; the idea is to find that activity that brings you out of the funk into the joy of another day. No excuses, no I don't have time, no that's silly, none, not one, like that old advertisement used to say "JUST DO IT!"

November 9, 2013

Another round of chemo down, doc says the CT scan showed significant reduction on the inner tumors. Another round scheduled for Thanksgiving week (bummer!). You gotta know I'm not myself when I'm off FB for a few days, LOL. Hanging out in my bed today, nursing a cup of peppermint tea and thinking about perusing some catalogs for Christmas presents. (If I can stay awake long enough) I know that this too shall pass, and fighting it won't make it go any quicker. Compared to what other chemo patients have to endure, I have nothing to complain about and I wish I could hold each and every one of them in my arms and let them know that I kinda have some idea of what they are going through, for it really cannot be put into words and unless you're projectile vomiting or broken out in some nasty rash there really aren't a lot of outward signs. Tis a lonely path this thing they call cancer...............

Observations by Janine- 2014

When Michelle made her first visit to my home after her leg was amputated, she wheeled up to my front door and then walked in. Of course, Henrietta the artificial leg was supporting her and she had the assistance of her walker. What was really funny was to watch all of us adults hovering as Shelli maneuvered up a step that we have into our living room

The twins, now four and a half, appraised the situation and quietly processed this change in Shelli. They saw first hand that Nana Shelli was walking with a gadget with a shoe attached at the end where her foot used to be. Without to much fan- fare, they welcomed her to the kitchen table with a big hug. They did ask to see her prosthesis and in their four year old way, they didn't dwell on the change they observed, instead, they quickly moved forward with smiles and acceptance. It is safe to say that

Liam and Julia have grown accustom to watching Nana Shelli walk around our house with her bionic leg.   I have developed a new awareness of the barriers that are presented to people who are in wheel chairs. Shelli and I can't visit many of our old favorite places; however we are busy discovering new, handicapped accessible places to enjoy our time together. I've also come to understand more fully how the experience of a cancer diagnosis is something that can't be imagined. Until those words, " you have cancer" are said to you, you are not able to feel the rush of emotions that are experienced by the cancer patient.

I also learned a lesson in not losing hope. Yes, my brother did not survive his physical battle with melanoma. However, I see now that the cancer experience as unique and individual as the cancer patient is. The outcomes of cancer diagnosis and treatment, though they have some predictability, can be as variable as the number of stars in the night sky.

Posts

January 02, 2014

Well here we are, two days into the New Year and I can guarantee that people are already becoming discouraged with their "New Year's Resolutions." When you wake up in the morning and everything is the same and you expected the mere fact that it's a new year to solve all your problems cause you made some silly ass empty promises to yourself, fully knowing that for the most part you're not going to follow through, of course you're going to be discouraged.

Change comes from within and no matter how good your intentions are, if you don't change the inside, nothing on the outside is going to change. Instead of making all those standard resolutions make ones that can and will change your life. How about promising to know yourself better so you can recognize the buttons that can be pushed and the areas that you tend to continue to do the same thing expecting different results. Maybe taking 5 minuets in the morning before you get out of bed to just be. Start training your mind to be quiet and commune with your inner self. Make this world a better place by making you a better person. To become a better person you have to work from the inside out. "Resolve" to become master of your thoughts and emotions, stop saying I can't, you can. Yes, it's hard and it takes real commitment. If you cannot commit to working at these inner changes they will fall short just as the false resolutions to change the outer do, for the reality is it's all up to you. Your thoughts, your emotions, your life. You have to understand that by doing this, the things going on around you will not change right away, what will change is how you handle these things. How you react, what you do and don't do, say and don't say, think and don't think these are the changes that will take place. Eventually the outer physical will change as well but to make that happen we have to start at square one, ourselves...HAPPY NEW YEAR TO ALL!

January 17, 2014

All the problems with Stumpy and the prosthetic were beginning to get me down. I want to be up and moving and I'm being blindsided at every turn. Then I got thinking, I bet there are things I can do without the prosthetic, like go up the stairs on my behind. I spoke to my PT and she was all for it. The first trip was truly that a "trip", but I made it! Today, we did it again and it was easier. Oh man, I can feel that shower cascading over me now; it's so close I can taste it. We still have a few things to figure out but I'm so happy to know I don't have to wait until I can navigate the stairs with Henrietta before I can take a shower. I haven't given up on using Henrietta on stairs by any means but till we can work together better, I have no problem hooching up the stairs on my butt. Another example of going with the flow and not letting what I think should be stand in the way of what can be done at the moment. I was so focused on using Henrietta that I totally forgot there might be another way for me to go up the stairs.

Do I like crawling around on the floor at 64 years old? Not particularly but hey it's what's available to me and I can do it, and I'm so grateful that I am flexible and limber enough to maneuver the steps, someone else probably would not be able to. The silver lining in the cloud................What was your silver lining today, I bet there was one and you didn't even notice it...........................

January 20, 2014

Are you constantly striving for perfection? Do you spend hours travelling from lot to lot to find the perfect Christmas tree? Do you reject buying something (other then clothing) that isn't perfect? Perfection is the job of the Universe and everything it creates is perfect. The images we have been subjected to from the moment we're born are ideals forced upon us by our ego driven lives and those who are so submersed in it they cannot see the perfection in everything. Every rose is perfect and beautiful, just as every human being is perfect and beautiful. We are trained to see flaws in everything, especially other humans. Then we happily spend thousands if not millions of dollars striving to reach that perfect image. I've seen people reject buying a beautiful knick knack because the paint job wasn't "perfect" and I saw it as unique and wonderful and couldn't understand rejecting something beautiful. Let's stop looking for the ego driven perfection and start seeing the perfection that exists.....................................

January 22, 2014

With all that I've been through and managed to keep my cool, the loss of my curls reduced me to tears......................... I had my hair cut yesterday and what I had feared was true, my beautiful curls are gone. They may grow back, I don't know. I do know that people who lose their hair from chemo have had it grow back better and even different colors, but to just lose the curls without losing the hair ? I dunno. Shows to go ya,

I do have a strong ego side despite myself. I realize there is nothing wrong in acknowledging these feelings and letting them out. The key is not to let them take over and make me go down the negative path. So for the moment I will mourn the loss of my beautiful curls and tomorrow I will try to figure out what to do with straight hair and how to make it look at least presentable. We cannot escape or deny our emotions, what we can do is understand where they are coming from and why and then control them and not let them control us. It would be so easy to use this as an excuse to see all the things I have "lost" over

112

the last 3 years and dwell on the negative side of this experience. But, I don't want to do that and even though my heart is broken (silly huh?) I understand that I cannot use it as a launching board to go down that dark and lonely road ....

January 29, 2014

Two thirds of the way through my last round of chemo (forever we pray), feeling chemoish (lol a new Shellism to add to the dictionary). Translation, I am very -very- very tired and not functioning so well. I did manage to stay up a little longer today than yesterday but as I sit here looking at the bed it is calling my name louder and louder so I believe I must obey and lay my weary body down. Love and hugs to all of you who have commented and liked my good news, it's wonderful to be able to share with so many caring people. Till the next time, God Speed my friends

January 31, 2014

One of the most difficult lessons to learn on this journey through the physical world is love. I'm not talking about romantic love; I'm talking about the love that is God. Unconditional, non judgmental, forgiving, accepting love. We are surrounded by people of all types and loving all of them is a monumental task. Our egos just keep getting in the way telling us

113

they should do this or that or act in the way we want them to or a bazillion other non loving commands.

It's easy to love those who are kind to us and act in a way that makes us happy and our egos agree with, but we are to love those that don't just as much. We don't have to like that person, or have that person in our life but it is imperative for our own personal growth that we learn to love those that are the hardest to love. We cannot grow nor learn to truly live the life that we were meant to live until we strip our ego entirely of its power and love everyone.

I struggle with this on a daily basis and am constantly reminding myself that the actions of these people and my reactions to them are all ego motivated and I have to consciously replace my negative reactions with thoughts of love and wellbeing for those people. Our ego jumps right in and justifies our negative thoughts with hundreds of reasons why we are right when we judge someone.

It is at this time s when you have to muster up all your strength and call upon the Universe to open up your heart and understand that it is not our job to do anything but love our fellow human beings and wish them well. I found an affirmation that has been of tremendous help to me that I would like to pass along; hopefully it will help some of you as well.

When faced with unloving thoughts, repeat to yourself "I lovingly place (persons name) in the hands of God. That which is for his/her own highest good shall come to him/her. Then let go. When the ego voice starts listing all the horrible things you want to happen to this person, just place them back in God's hands again, and let go.......................

February 2, 2014

When things are going "bad" and life seems intolerable, do you seek out those who will wallow in the unfairness of life with you or do you gravitate toward those who are positive and uplifting? Unfortunately, most people will head for someone to wallow with. Someone who has major problems of their own and loves to talk about them and wallow in the negative. The old saying "misery loves company" is a truth.

We become the misery, make it our story, and just keep attracting more and more cause like attracts like and whatever vibes you are putting out to the Universe will attract more of the same. As humans we tend to want to have a companion in misery, someone who "understands how much life sucks and how unfair it is" and someone who will listen as we list all the horrible things life is throwing at us and how miserable we are. If someone won't play the poor me game you tend to stay away from them, they don't understand, they have no compassion; their life is going fine so you have nothing in common any more.

Positive people will listen to you but will not feed into the negative. They may even piss you off by trying to point out the positive in your life (yes, no matter what is going on there is still positive around you, but you have to acknowledge it or sooner or later it too will fall to the wayside). Again here's that horrible word "choice". You can choose NOT to wallow. You can choose to find the good and hang on to it with all your might as your ego slams you with all the black thoughts. Chose to NOT hang on to those thoughts, just watch them as they go through your mind, like a conveyor belt, you don't have to take them off and play with them, you can just let them pass by and chose those thoughts that make you feel better, that acknowledge what good is around you. You will attract what you give your attention to, are you going to chose to wallow or will you chose the brighter path...

February 06, 2014

The past-we all have one but how we remember and what we do with it are important factors in the journey to peace and love. Do you go to the past to relive pleasant memories and indulge in a few moments of nostalgia or do you relive all the wrongs that have been done to you? I remember my mom getting all worked up and angry over a friend who borrowed a sweater and got a stain on it over 50 years ago!!!!! OMG, how can you hang on to that stuff???? Why would you? All those resentments and blaming others for the wrongs in your life are akin to cancer. They literally eat away at you, holding you in a place of non-forgiveness and stop the flow of love that the Universe wants to bestow upon you.

Again, it all boils down to choice. You can chose to hang on to all the wrongs that have happened, wishing ill will upon those whose hurt you or you can grow and understand that forgiveness is the only way to go. You don't have to "physically go and embrace that person or situation" but you do have to forgive and let it go. Right now, think of a person who you perceived did you a wrong. What happens to you? Do the hackles on the back of your neck bristle? Does your body tense up and your heart beat a little faster? Right there you should realize how harmful these feelings you are harboring are to you. Mentally say "I forgive you" and keep saying it until your body responds and finds a calmer and more peaceful place. I find that repeating these words of Catherine Ponder, "I forgive everyone and everything in my past, present, and future that could possibly need forgiving. I forgive them and they forgive me. All things are made right between us." every day, is a truly helpful and powerful affirmation. You don't follow it up with all the terrible things you want to happen to them, you let go. This is not done for anyone but you. It doesn't affect the other person, it is entirely for you to learn to let go of the past and learn that forgiveness is another word for peace, for without forgiveness there can be no peace and without peace there can be no love and without love there can be no you.....................................

February 08, 2014

When I was a child I used to think the dandelion seeds were fairies. They would be flying all over and so small and delicate and really somewhat shaped like a fairy that I was totally convinced they were indeed fairies. The other day I was sitting outside waiting for my friend to maneuver her car around so I could get in and I saw one a dandelion seed. Mind you, now it's the beginning of February, we're up to our knees in snow and it's been extremely cold. There are no dandelions out. Where did that piece of fluff come from and why was I in the right place at the right time to see it. As silly as it sounds my first reaction was "Oh look, there's a fairy." It disappeared as quickly as it came, I tried to find it but I could not. Now I'm not trying to convince you that I saw a fairy but illustrating what wonders you can find if you open your eyes and pay attention. I can guarantee that if there were other people in that same situation, they would have never noticed. There was something special in my dandelion seed sighting. It brought a smile to my face and a warm glow in my heart. It felt like a connection with the child Shelli and a time when life was no so complicated and fairies did indeed exist..............

February 9, 2014

I saw a post where someone asked "If you could spend one hour on this bench with anyone living or dead, who would you chose?" I have pondered this for days. Many people chose loved ones, mom, dad, grandpa, others chose great spiritual or political leaders the list was as varied as it was impressive. I finally made my decision. I would spend that hour with me, my spiritual self-stripped of all ego and material concerns. She would know where my weak spots are and could tell me how to strengthen them; she would know where I am strong and how to put those qualities to best use. She could guide me through the remainder of my trip through this physical existence and help me to become what I should be. I would be able to find out what I should be doing and how I should be doing it and give me the insight to myself that we all need.

Because she is spirit and we are all one in spirit she would encompass all those others as well. I could once again feel my mother and father's love, I could avail myself of the wisdom of Jesus, the Dalai Lama ,anyone I could possibly think of would be there as well. An hour would hardly be enough time but it sure would be an incredible hour!!!!!

February 12, 2014

Have you ever just been bopping along through your day, doing what you do and not really thinking about anything in particular when a feeling of excited anticipation comes over you? That happened to me today. There's definitely a ripple in the force and it's producing some extraordinary events that will be wonderful for me and I believe others as well. It's like when you're at the fireworks and they let loose with that one that booms so loud you can feel it in your chest. My whole body is vibrating with anticipation. This came out of nowhere, nothing has happened to indicate any changes or good news but my energy field is all atwitter (not sure that's a word). If I could dance I would (guess I'll have to settle for the bunny hop lol). The best way to describe it is to compare it to Scrooge when he woke up on Christmas morning and found out he was still alive. (lol I have a vision of Alistair Sim standing on his head when the cleaning lady come in). Maybe my body is just catching up to the good news from the PET Scan, (that I am cancer free) but I don't think so. What an incredible life this is!!!

Conclusion

Shelli

Positive thinking and the act of giving thanks brings real physical results. Knowing how and why it works isn't necessary and will not affect the outcome of serious applications of these laws. It's like turning on a light switch, as long as the connection is good and you are plugged in, the light will go on. Not many of us understand the properties of electricity or how and why it works, yet we can still flip a switch and the lights will go on. You cannot expect the light to go on if it's unplugged or has faulty wiring or the power is out.

Changing your thinking and being truly grateful requires the same attention to detail. You don't have to worry about there being no power or the power going out. The laws of the universe are always working. The power is always on. Every time you send out a heartfelt thank you, you are plugging into that power. A light goes on. In the beginning it may be so dim and far away that you can barely see it, but I assure you that it is there. Each positive thought strengthens the connection and the light becomes brighter and brighter. Of course, we can't forget that there is also a negative side to this energy. Our goal is to emit more positive than negative.

Conclusion

Janine

How many times have we exclaimed, we don't have time for the disruptions that occur in our lives? The disruptions come in many different forms; including illness

I ask you, can a catastrophic life threatening illness spark a spiritual quest? I would answer, absolutely, and it is very evident that Shelli is succeeding on the quest for peace in her soul. There is no doubt in my mind that those who practice the type of life philosophy that Shelli has written about over the past four years, the philosophy of acknowledging hurts or offenses, forgiving them and then letting them go, create for themselves an aura or energy force of peacefulness and acceptance.

Does one ever really settle into life as cancer survivor? I think everyone who has had the diagnosis of cancer strives to regain some sense of normalcy- a new normalcy as a survivor and Shelli has done just that.

When you think about it, from the moment we are born, the clock starts counting down to our last days in our physical life form. Elizabeth Kubler – Ross notes "dying is something we human beings do continuously, not just at the physical ends of our lives on this earth". I leave you with this question; don't we owe it to our souls to make each precious moment count?

I'm grateful l for the presence of Shelli in my life. I'm grateful for the opportunity to learn more about the power of forgiveness. I'm grateful for the hummingbird that visits my bee balm daily.